What We Do

Working in the Theatre

by

BO METZLER

(A.E.A., I.A. Local #764, I.A. Local #1)

Awarded the 2008 Book of the Year
Gold Medal for Performing Arts / Drama
by
FOREWORD MAGAZINE

Illustrations by

Rob Hamilton

Infinity Publishing.com

ISBN 0-7414-5004-6

Published by:

INFINITY
PUBLISHING.COM

1094 New DeHaven Street, Suite 100
West Conshohocken, PA 19428-2713
Info@buybooksontheweb.com
www.buybooksontheweb.com
Toll-free (877) BUY BOOK
Local Phone (610) 941-9999
Fax (610) 941-9959

Printed in the United States of America

Published June 2009

For my mother who inspired me and let me be.

And for all my fellow theatre people
who do what we do
for the love, the dream and the applause.

The author, young and green,
attempting Shakespeare in
A Midsummer Night's Dream
(1968; age 17)

PRE-SHOW
(Preface)

In the theatre, the "Pre-show" is a show before the show.
It is mainly a Dinner Theater custom where
the waiters and waitresses become performers
and sing a few songs, tell a few jokes or put on a skit.
It occurs while the audience finishes their meal
while the dishes are cleared and everyone settles down
for the evening's main event.
A "Pre-show" can happen on any special evening where,
for instance, there may be an author to launch,
a charity to fund, a dignitary to honor,
a grand opening or a world premiere.
Whether it's entertainment or honor, it all happens
before the main show—as a warm-up to the main
event.

Here the "Pre-show" takes on a slightly different form.
Instead of speeches or jokes or songs . . .
we will begin with a little "how it all began" story
which will explain the reason this book was written.

So . . . may I have the house lights dimmed to half,
and my follow spot, please?

The idea for this book actually took root around
1980 when I was visiting my hometown in Ohio
for the Christmas Holidays. This was my traditional week-
long visit with parents, siblings and friends, highlighted by

the opportunity to partake in a juicy Yuletide turkey which I so looked forward to each year. The food, the family and the fun had become an annual affair ever since I left my hometown six years earlier to seek my fame and fortune. And, amid the revelry, there were the usual curious questions about what I was up to and how things were going in the "big city" of New York.

"What are you working on now?" asks one cousin.

"Well, nothing at the moment," was my self conscious reply.

"Aren't there any auditions? You were always such a good actor."

"Yes, there are always auditions," I explained. "Unfortunately there is also, always, a lot of competition."

"What do you do, just go around to each theater to see if they are auditioning?"

"Well," I smile, "there are several trade papers which list audition notices and, in New York, you don't generally audition in a theater."

Seeing the question marks all over his face, I tried to explain. "You see, in New York, most theaters are just empty spaces for rent, like apartments or warehouses. When a show is going to be produced, it's up to the producer of that show to rent a theater that will accommodate his needs. And generally, even though theaters are contracted months in advance, move-in dates aren't scheduled until after the show has hired a cast and they are already in rehearsal."

"So you need to see the producer, then? Where do they have the auditions?"

"Well, the producer doesn't handle casting. Not directly. The director or a casting director does. And auditions can take place in the casting director's office or, very often, in a rented rehearsal studio."

And so it went, again—the explanations. I tried to be as simple and concise as possible. I tried very hard to use words that were easily understood—because I am well aware of the fact that I can lapse into a familiar "theatre-ease" dialect which many non-theatre people still don't quite understand. Invariably, no matter how cautious I attempted to be; no matter where I started my explanations, there was always something missing. There was always some little tidbit of background information, not explained, that was crucial to a current explanation. Things would usually get confusing as I would go back and explain something else which would result in my losing track of what it was that I began to explain in the first place.

To complicate everything, each year I was coming home with new stories about new experiences in new areas of the theatre that I was getting involved in. Early in my career, when I wasn't finding much work as an actor, I was also taking work as a stage manager as well as backstage as a stagehand—hanging lights and building scenery. So each year, with every new experience, my explanations began to get slightly more confusing. This usually prompted the most frequent question—the one I've heard more times than I can count. It is my all-time favorite:

"What is it, exactly, that you do?"

"I am a stage manager," I would answer, chest held high (when stage managing was my main area of concentration).

"Oh . . . I see . . ." a polite lie. "I thought you were an actor."

"Well, I was . . . that is, I am . . . I mean . . . I started as an actor, when I first went to New York. And I still have an itch to be onstage. But while I'm not acting, I do other things to make ends meet. And because I sometimes work as a stagehand and even as a dresser, I found that the job of managing the stage was something I was well equipped to do."

There were several years when my varied resume was a splendid source of total confusion.

"Why don't you do a TV commercial?"

I can't tell you how many times I've heard that one—especially during the period when I was modeling.

Or . . .

"Why don't you get a part on one of those soap operas? You could make a lot of money doing that."

"To tell you the truth, I wish I could. But it's not that easy."

"Oh . . ."

And so it went: questions, followed by explanations, followed by confusion, followed by more explanations. It became terribly frustrating and sometimes even a bit exhausting. There I was, year after year, trying to explain the crazy, mixed-up life that I had chosen for myself, and I usually got nowhere fast. Undaunted, I endured. The explanations were too brief, usually outdated (since I was always doing something different) and they happened only once a year. No wonder I got so many blank looks. My poor family . . . I don't blame them.

I had to figure out a way to make the explanations better—more current, continuous and as complete as possible. I could make more frequent trips home with updates, but that would become prohibitively expensive. Frequent long distance phone calls would also add to my already overburdened budget. Not a good idea (this was before cell phones with free long distance). Maybe I could write letters (before email), constantly updating my career and life with lengthy explanations. The thought of words like "constantly" and "lengthy" made my hand hurt.

And then it hit me! Wait a minute!

What about *one* lengthy explanation? What about writing down everything I could think of that related to the business I was in, and all of the jobs I have had, and make copies of it for everyone who wanted them? I could share my experiences, with all the peculiarities and manifestations, and hopefully be finished with all the repetitive explaining—once and for all!

What a great idea! Simple enough, right?

As I thought about it, the solution became simple too. A book! I'd write a book about the theatre and then, on the next visit home for Christmas, I'd give a copy of the book to everyone who asked any questions.

The aim of the book would be to explain everything in theatre—what everyone did and how all the aspects of the theatre related to each other. A simple, concise, general explanation—a kind of reference book, so to speak, with terms defined, job descriptions explained and relationships and methodologies explored. The book would translate the language of theatre into the language of family and friends—so that everyone would understand.

The book would not be a "how to" book explaining *how* to do theatre, because many people have written these books already—covering all areas of the business. It *would,* however, be a who, what and where type book—an insider's view of the theatre, relating what I saw, what I did, and what I learned through my own experiences. It would be an explanation of the fundamentals of theatre so that any reader could begin to see, understand and appreciate the life that theatre people live as they pursue their careers.

There are probably thousands of people all over the country—my fellow theatre people and their family and friends—who are experiencing communication difficulties similar to mine when trying to understand the life and the business of theatre. Maybe my book would help explain things for them.

And as I thought further, I realized that there are tens of thousands of college students contemplating a career in the theatre—each semester of each year. A comprehensive and practical book outlining the scope of professional theatre would be a helpful and maybe even necessary addition to every intro-to-theatre or theatre appreciation course in the curriculum. I wish a book like this had existed when I went to college.

Was I biting off more than I could chew? Was I thinking too big? I thought not. After all . . . people with far less practical experience in the theatre than me have written shelves of theatre books. Why couldn't I? And if people could benefit from my sharing what I have experienced—why shouldn't I give it a try?

It took me over 30 years to write this book because first I had to live it and experience it. And as I publish this book I am passing my 34th year in New York and in the professional theatre. I have worked in almost every theatrical arena in and out of New York (Off-Off-Broadway to Tours to Children's Theatre); I have held nearly every job on stage or backstage (acting, stage managing, carpentry, props, electrics and wardrobe); I have written for the stage as well as produced for the stage; I have driven scenery trucks as well as coordinated limousine transportation; I have worked in TV and on Broadway (including on the 3 longest running Broadway hits). So who better to write about all of the different jobs in the theatre, and how they relate to each other, than someone who has actually done pretty much everything in the theatre at one time or another? Proudly and yet humbly I answer: "I'm your guy!"

So here it is. A first-hand comprehensive compilation of what I have observed, learned, experienced and accomplished while working in the theatre business. It's organized into chapters and sections that will help anyone who reads it understand the ins and outs of the theatre. It explores the language, the jobs, the venues, the training, the relationships, the activities, the sweat, the toil, the stress, the fun, the people, the camaraderie, the good times and the not so good times—all about what we do working in the theatre.

I'm sure I have forgotten or missed a few things—or been occasionally redundant. And, since the business is always changing, there may be things I did and ways I did them that may seem antiquated to future readers. So I will probably update the book from time to time. But it is my intention that this one, long, detailed explanation is basic yet universal enough so that everyone who reads it will get something out of it—whether they are coming from no knowledge or from an already established career. And hopefully it is concise and informative enough so that anyone in the theatre, planning to go into the theatre, or anyone who knows someone who is in the theatre, can begin to communicate with knowledge, understanding and appreciation.

It is in this regard that I have set about this curious task. It may at times be personal—with anecdotes from my life and my experiences—but it is every theatre person's life and every theatre person's experiences. We all want you, our family, friends, and future theatre people to know what we do. In fact we need you to know—so that we can share our experiences and enjoy them together.

So relax and get comfortable. I hope that you enjoy what you are about to read as much as I've enjoyed living it for you.

Does everyone have a program? (If not, turn the page.)

Follow spot fades to black.
Hopefully, there is polite applause.

The house lights fade to black.
A hush of excitement and anticipation
wafts over the crowd.
A few people take one more glance at The Program.

The main show is about to begin!

THE PROGRAM
(Table of Contents)

PROLOGUE
(Introduction)

In the theatre, the "Prologue" is a kind of preview
or introduction.
It is always necessary whenever it is included.
Sometimes it supplies the audience with some needed
background information,
or an introduction of characters,
or a foreshadowing of events to come.

The "Prologue" is presented by
the same cast of characters,
in the same surroundings.
It is short and to the point,
and leads directly to the main event.

Shakespeare loved the "Prologue."

So . . .
Curtain up, Go . . . Light Cue 1, Go!

Let me start by saying that the information and explanations in this book pertain, for the most part, to the theatre business as it exists in New York City—proudly and subjectively referred to as "The Theatre Capital of the World." This is where, arguably, the best professional theatre is presented. And this is where up-to-date theatre methodologies and technologies are developed and practiced to their full potential. This doesn't mean, however, that theatre is different in other places. It is not. Generally speaking, theatre is theatre everywhere you go, anywhere in the world. There is a fundamental universal language of theatre and common universal procedures and applications. Some techniques may vary and some personnel may have different job descriptions or titles, but at the core, it is still the same theatre.

It should also be pointed out that a single book on theatre could never say everything there is to be said on the subject. There are already hundreds of books on bookstore shelves dealing with dozens of different aspects of theatre. Most of these books have a specific point-of-view and deal with specific areas of concentration. Many of these books tell you *how* to do things—like *how* to act or *how* to build scenery. This book is a little different. I am being specific only in the sense that I am dealing with the subject of theatre. My intention, however, is to approach the subject and discussion of theatre from a *general* point-of-view and deal with *all* the fundamental aspects of theatre in a universal way. I have written the book especially with the non-theatre person, or the theatre person-to-be, in mind. I believe, also, that even working theatre people will get something out of it.

What you will get here is an overview of the theatre, as a business, as an occupation, as a life style and even as a dream. We'll explore where plays come from and how they get produced. Describe the kinds of people who work in the theatre, and a little of what they do. Find out how actors, directors, stage managers and others, look for work, keep their jobs and what they do when they are out of work. We'll also look at the different types of theaters and theatre companies, and wherever possible, point out and explain the similar and contrasting features that make theatre anywhere the same—yet different. We'll even outline a typical audition situation, take a look at an average rehearsal day and watch a load-in and a work call. In essence, a basic, fundamental, behind-the-scenes exploration of the who, what, where and maybe even why of theatre life in New York.

It may get a bit confusing at times. But once you get the hang of it, the world and the language of the theatre will become second nature to you. This book may not change theatre, but it will certainly help a lot more people understand it.

If you are a career theatre person then you are probably well acquainted with nearly everything in this book, but maybe not. Read on, for you may discover a greater appreciation of theatre and of the variety of people who make it a career. If nothing else, you can give this book to a family member or a friend and once and for all let them know what you do.

If you are new to the business yet already possess a basic familiarity with the subject matter, consider this a preparatory or refresher course that will further enhance your present knowledge.

If you are a student of theatre, then I assume a certain interest or infatuation has brought you this far. Welcome. Let our adventure help to bring the theatre world into focus for you. It may help guide you on the right path in a theatrical career.

For any reader who is venturing into the world of the theatre for the first time, my warmest greetings! I am pleased that you are taking the time to discover and to understand our world. I hope your trip will be a memorable one.

Whatever the reasons you have opened this book— WELCOME!

Now, without any further delay, let's roll up our sleeves and dig right in with some basic fundamental definitions to help guide you through this experience.

Anticipating a variety of readers with knowledge and familiarity ranging from absolutely nothing to possibly a great deal, it was tricky deciding on a point-of-view that could be appreciated by everyone. I decided on a rather basic approach—that of a conversation between friends or family members—which mirrors the reason I began writing this book. It is my hope that this will give everyone a welcoming feeling and keep hardly anything from going unexplained or being misunderstood as we travel on our journey.

And so we will begin by defining four terms that seem simple on the surface, but can, and do, cause occasional mild confusion. These terms are basic to any discussion of the theatre. And because of their somewhat interchangeable, ambiguous natures, we must come to a temporary meeting of the minds as to their definitions.

1) **THE THEATRE** — A genre term or universal expression used to describe any performance of a script, by live performers, in front of a live audience. In essence: the Dramatic Art; the Theatre World. People who are engaged in "the theatre" are called "theatre people." Theatre people call it "the business."

Not to be confused with:

2) **A THEATER** — The place where the live performance happens. It doesn't always have a stage, or seats, or even a roof or walls. But it is always a "theater" and it is the place where "theatre" happens.

Notice the spelling of these two terms. You probably thought that I couldn't make up my mind which to use. In actual fact, the two spellings (the first European, the second American) can be used interchangeably, with either definition. I have designated them in this way only as a means of distinguishing between them to avoid confusion on our journey.

3) **THE SHOW** — The activity that the live performers are engaged in onstage at the "theater." The "show" can be a drama like *Hamlet*; a comedy like *The Odd Couple*; or a musical like *Fiddler on the Roof*. The "show" can also be an act like *Seinfeld on Broadway* or an extravaganza like the *Radio City Christmas Spectacular*. Some synonyms include: "the play," "the production," "the job," or simply "work."

When a theatre person is engaged in some activity on a "show," he or she is said to be "working on a show," or "doing a show," or that he or she "has a show."

Almost every "show" can be performed in almost every "theater" (with some scenery adjustments). Sometimes a single "show" is performed at several different "theaters," one after another, on a weekly or monthly basis (called a "tour"). Any "show" can have multiple casts and staffs who may alternate at different performances. Or there may be duplicate productions of the same "show" being performed by different performers, simultaneously, at different "theaters."

4) **THE ACTOR** — A term that can (and does in this book) refer to both male and female performers. The feminine version—actress—is typically no longer used. The status of "professional" is applied to any "actor" who is in the serious pursuit of a "theatre" career. You do not actually have to earn money to be considered a "professional" actor. Lots of different types of people work on a "show" or in a "theater." They are all called "theatre people" and they may all be "professionals," but they are not all "actors."

Basic stuff, right? There's much more. You'll soon be able to look back at all the new information and explanations and say, "Now I understand!"

There is one other point that should be addressed before we continue: which is the use of *personal pronouns.* Whenever one deals with subject matter that involves many different people in general categorical terms, one is bound to use personal pronouns frequently. And there are a lot of them in this book. Fundamentally, in the theatre business, any and all jobs, positions, distinctions and theories are held or attributed to both male and female theatre people. I have chosen to use specific pronouns as they correspond to my actual theatrical experiences, because as I wrote about types of people I often had specific people in mind. This helped me keep track of references. The fact that "he" is more frequently used than "she" is pure coincidence. I have also chosen *not* to use the term "he/she" because it is awkward and interrupts the flow of the sentence.

Now let us back up a bit.
Which came first? The chicken or the egg? The "actor" or the "show?"
To avoid a debate, I'll say the "show" came first. And where does the show come from? It comes from the "writer."
Now let us begin...

The lights dip to black.
Perhaps some polite applause.

There may be an appropriate sound effect
like crashing thunder.
Maybe some scenery gets changed.

All the "participants" are in their place.
Standby!

Lights up—GO!

ACT I :
WHO AND WHAT

Scene 1: THE WRITER

The Writer may be ensconced in a sparsely furnished New York City apartment which overlooks some famous landmark, street, or, in all likelihood, alleyway. There are sounds of traffic and sirens on the outside, and occasional creaks from the walls, floors, neighbors, or the cat on the inside. He is seated on a broken yet sturdy office chair and poised majestically in front of him, on a paper-littered desk, is his computer. (When I first started writing this book I was using a Smith Corona Selectric).

Close at hand are a half-filled can of warm soda, a half-empty box of Wheat Thins, and several Post-It notes stuck on the computer monitor. Interruptions abound—the teenage son needs money, the phone rings with another credit card offer and the next door neighbor needs to "borrow" two aspirin.

The Writer is dressed in shorts and a T-shirt, no shoes or socks and a three-day growth on his face. (And you really don't want to get too close to him if you know what I mean). He is writing.

The words are coming in dribs and drabs . . . the scenes are being created . . . the dialogue is taking shape . . . the characters are coming to life . . . the pages are getting filled . . . and despite the interruptions, the work is getting done.

Writing is a lonely life, a solitary life, and a painful life—especially around the neck, back and shoulders. But the Writer, living within his script, feels only the reality he is creating. He is meeting people, talking to them, sharing relationships, hardships, joy, love, and anger—even hatred. And for the talented Writer who perseveres and endures, there is the hope that his enterprise, his creation, his "child" will be born a masterpiece leading to fame, fortune and even awards. Not to mention the personal satisfaction of simply completing a piece of work—which for any artist is an unparalleled personal achievement.

Using only the alphabet, the English language (in our case) and a few punctuation marks, the Writer creates what can easily be called a work of art. Words are his brushes and colors; his lenses and film; his chisels and stone; or his clay and wheel. And in his mind is an idea.

Where it all begins

A story, a person, a happening, a memory, a dream, a sadness, a joy, a hope—an idea!

The Writer puts human existence into words. He tells us about the life we live everyday, but never stop to notice. He gives us a glimpse of a special person that we miss, or that we may have never known. He recalls for us an event that has slipped by far too quickly. He digs deep and brings back that moment from long ago that we have always cherished. He reminds us of that wish or desire that we almost forgot. He makes us feel the pain again, and feel the ecstasy. He may, with his words, fortify our very reasons for waking up . . . for going on.

You never thought of it that way? Well, ponder this: What would it be like without the Writer? What would it be like without nursery rhymes from Mother Goose or stories from Dr. Seuss or Rudyard Kipling? What would it be like without novels from Hemingway, Tolstoy, Steinbeck, Sandberg or Rowling? What would it be like without plays from Shakespeare, Shaw, Brecht, Williams or O'Neill?

What would it be like if an actor got up on the stage and had nothing to say? Even the great mime Marcel

Marceau has a story idea for each of his pantomimes and improvisational actors have outlines that help guide them through suggestions from an audience. Without the *idea*, and some sort of script, the actor has nothing to work from— nowhere to go.

If there is nothing for the actor to do, there will be nothing to see.

If there is nothing to see, there will be no audience.

If there is no audience, there is no theatre.

And without theatre . . . well, for one thing, I wouldn't be writing this book.

Obviously, for our purposes, we are concentrating on the Writer who is writing scripts for the theatre.

There are dramatic scripts and comedy scripts and musical scripts. Dramatic scripts are usually serious but sometimes funny. Comedy scripts are filled with laughs as well as poignancy. And musical scripts (called "the book"), together with the music and lyrics, make up a musical.

Most scripts tell very traditional stories of people that we can usually identify with. These stories, fact or fiction, structured into acts and scenes, are told through monologues, or dialogue between characters, or lyrics of songs.

Some scripts may be very stylized or surrealistic, with very little dialogue, telling a tale of the mind or spirit. A monologue is a script for a show with only one character. And a script for a mime may be just a series of short notes. Ideally the intention is that the script becomes a show, performed by actors, in front of a live audience—making theatre.

My own first venture into writing for the theatre happened by accident while I was still in college. I wrote a play about Abraham Lincoln and his wife Mary Todd entitled *Abraham and Mary.* The idea for my play grew out of a brief appearance in another play where I dressed like Lincoln attending a costume ball. Working with a costume and some make-up, I shockingly discovered that I could actually look convincingly like Abe.

Well, this representation progressed after the show closed, when I decided to dress like Abe on his birthday and walk around the campus telling Lincoln anecdotes and stories. This developed, finally, into my writing a script so that I could fully portray him onstage. I was able to produce the play later that year as an independent study project in the theatre department; as well as several years later in New York as part of a One Act Festival of New Playwrights.

Unfortunately, however, all scripts do not automatically become shows. There are some scripts that are never even finished. Some scripts lie dormant, relegated to oblivion on a floppy disk, a shelf or a file drawer because the Writer was unsatisfied. Still others, read, tried and even tested, just don't stand up to criticism.

Writing as a career, is a tremendous challenge. Not only does it require a certain amount of intelligence, but it also requires an abundance of imagination. Ideas can be easy. Putting them down on paper, in words that convey emotions, takes as much resilience, perseverance and determination as it does skill.

The Writer, writing for the theatre, has much to consider. Aside from the story itself, the Writer will consider the audience as he writes. He may wish to teach them, or admonish them; warn them, or poke fun at them. He may even set out to intentionally insult them. Many Writers spend time describing scenery, costumes, lights and props in an effort to further define the world they wish to create. Some may even have certain actors in mind when they write their dialogue.

A Writer must also have patience—patience with himself in order to allow his imagination to work and patience from those around him who share his life. Writers can get crazy sometimes. They work at all hours and not always at the computer. Sometimes it's a matter of just staring out the window—thinking. And when the words finally start coming, they must be written down—whether it's 12 noon or 3 am.

Then there is the most dreaded of all diseases—writer's block! A Writer can go for days, months or even years, without a single syllable down on paper. That's when the anger, frustration and doubt creep in. That's also when patience is a vital virtue, because there is nothing to be done, except wait—until the ideas begin to flow again.

No one forces a Writer to write. For the most part he must be self-motivated. From idea to outline; from the first draft to the fifth or even the tenth; from word processor to stage, the Writer must find his own motivation to see his work through to the end, and to give birth to his creation. Between the first piece of paper or blank computer screen and that longed for opening night; through suggestion after suggestion from friends, relatives, editors, actors, directors and producers; and change after change during re-writes and rehearsals, that little idea that long ago germinated in the Writer's mind goes through an incredible gestation period. Only maybe during the final week before opening night will a script be called finished, but even after opening and after reviews are published there may be more revisions. It can be a never ending process.

No matter how long it takes to write, whether it is produced on stage or not, or how successful it is—it always starts with an idea. And this idea becomes theatre thanks to the Writer.

The Composer / Lyricist

As you probably know, a script with songs and music is called a "musical." The Writer of the musical script is called the Book Writer. The Writer of the music is called a Composer. The Writer of the lyrics is called the Lyricist.

Sometimes the Composer is also the Lyricist. Sometimes the Book Writer also writes the lyrics. Usually, when a musical is being written, at least two people are working on it. The Book Writer writes all of the dialogue, the Composer handles the music and they may even collaborate on the lyrics.

Have you heard of Gilbert and Sullivan; or Lerner and Lowe; or Rodgers and Hart? Have you heard of Tim Rice and Andrew Lloyd Webber? How about Tim Rice and Sir Elton John? These are a few of the teams who have collaborated on many of the greatest Broadway musicals.

Just as the secluded Writer hammers out his scripts on a word processing keyboard, the Composer, usually also working in a vacuum, spends many solitary hours plucking the keys on *his* keyboard—a piano. He is at work on his own *idea*, possibly dreamed up with a Writer. And while the Writer tells his story through words, the Composer tinkers with melodies and harmonies and explores special poignant moments that may be highlighted with music. They can be dramatic moments, emotional moments, character development or plot development moments. These moments become songs and musical interludes.

The Composer's music comes from inspirations and ideas that are as different for each Composer as the ideas and inspirations are for Writers. His melodies are little snippets of music that may come to him at odd times during the day or night. His thematic harmonies may take weeks or months to work out. He plucks his keys over and over again until songs emerge. He fiddles with them and tunes them. He may add some words and sing them. After great effort, all of the inspiration and dedicated work becomes a score for a musical.

Most scores are written on the piano and later orchestrated to include other instruments. Just as the Writer writes with scenery and costumes in mind, the Composer works with an orchestra in mind as he "hears" the notes and the sounds of the other instruments. The notes and instruments are the language of the Composer. Each instrument is a character with a voice. The goal is a collaboration of these instrumental voices which is the finished score of the musical.

The Composer helps to tell the story. His music and the lyrics are part of the dialogue. The characters speak and sing as the audience listens. Dramatic tension is created by music. Humor is created by music. Music and lyrics are sometimes used to reveal the thoughts of the actors. It all goes hand in hand, piece by piece, telling the story.

As with any play, not every musical gets seen or heard. And even in a finished musical not all of the songs that were written make it to opening night, while some are added at the last minute—like Stephen Sondheim's "Send in the Clowns" from *A Little Night Music* that was written in two days and added during the rehearsal process.

Even though in any typical Broadway season there are more musicals than straight plays on view, far more were written than ever saw the light of day. The Broadway musical has been entertaining audiences for decades and will continue to inspire Writers and Composers to develop the next idea.

I have never written music. I don't even play a musical instrument, though I have always wished I could. I have sung music—in the shower, in the car, as well as on stage. Most of my musical performing happened back in college musicals, but once I appeared on a Broadway stage, back in the days when stage managers could understudy performers. This happened during my first Broadway show called *Marlowe,* when too many people were out sick and I had to "go on" in a minor role. I even contributed a line of lyrics to one of the songs—but I would hardly call myself a Lyricist.

Back in the late 70s I began writing the book for a musical based on the life of Phyllis Wheatley, America's first black poet. A friend was going to write the music but the project never materialized and the book was relegated to my filing cabinet where it remains to this day.

Over the years, I have been around a few of the best musicals that have ever graced the Broadway stage. Aside from setting up chairs, instruments and music stands in numerous orchestra pits, I have listened to the scores of these shows on a nightly basis, and I have developed an appreciation for the craft of molding words and music into a cohesive dramatic product that thrills audiences and is indeed an art form. There isn't and never will be anything like the Broadway musical with live musicians in an orchestra pit.

Writing and composing are how one begins every play or musical. After all of this inspiration and work, after all of the collaboration and achievement, just how do these plays or musicals get from computer screen and music sheet to the theater stage? Remember that scripts don't automatically become shows just because they are written. Something must happen to them—some strange, unique and convoluted process of transformation must occur. This transformation is the essence of the "magic" of theatre.

In order for a script to become a show, it has to be "produced." Webster defines "produce" thusly: "To bring to view; offer for inspection; to get ready and present on the stage."

One who "produces," also according to Webster, is called a "Producer."

Scene 2: THE PRODUCER

In the beginning, as we have seen, there was a script. And a Producer found it and read it, and the Producer was pleased and said that it was good, and the script began its journey toward becoming a show.

This allusion to other well-known almighty activities is not accidental. In the professional theatre, the Producer is the big man, the top banana, the boss of bosses, the one who hires, the one who fires and the final last word. He is the person who makes everything go, and he can, likewise, make everything stop—at any time.

Along with all of this power comes a great deal of responsibility. Not only is the Producer responsible for making sure everything goes well, he is also responsible for things not going well. He can take all the praise when his show is a hit. And he must ultimately take the blame when his show tanks and closes on opening night. This is a tremendous burden and the main reason for the fact that there are very few successful Producers.

Technically, anyone can be a Producer. It's true. Your uncle can be a Producer. Your mother's beautician can be a Producer. Your brother-in-law's golfing partner can be a Producer. Anyone can be a Producer as long as they possess two basic things: 1) a show and 2) lots of money.

In any given Broadway season, a fair number of the people listed as Producer in various show programs have never produced a show before in their lives. Some of them got lucky and scored a hit. Some of them should have stayed out of the business.

There is no school to attend in order to learn how to be a Producer. Producers come from different places. Many were former directors, general managers, stage managers, actors or even writers who wanted, or needed, a career change. Others had money and may have been looking for a tax shelter, or perhaps had a spouse, lover or child who wanted to be in a show.

All Producers who work on Broadway must abide by certain labor agreements and regulations set down by The League of American Theatres and Producers which functions as their bargaining group in negotiations with all the different theatrical Unions. Independent Producers who are not actual members of the League, like Disney, follow the League guidelines but negotiate their own contracts.

Anyone can be *called* a Producer—for whatever reason. But truly *being* a Producer—especially a good one— is not a simple matter. There are four basic characteristics that every Producer should possess and the greater the degree of these characteristics, the greater chance for success for the Producer.

The Characteristics of a Producer

First, the Producer should have a good working knowledge of general business. Remember, theatre is also called "show *business*," and it is truthfully that—a business. Producing a show is like running a small, incorporated business with offices, staff, payroll, bills and problems—not the least of which is finding investors and raising money. If there is no money—there is no show!

Second, the Producer should know enough about theatre in general, and all its aspects, in order to be able to choose wisely the different people who will help him achieve the success he strives for. These people—directors, designers, actors, etc.—are the bread and butter of the business, and if the Producer makes wrong choices in his staff, it could prove fatal.

Third, it is the Producer's responsibility to pick the show. And, just as a bad script doesn't always mean failure, a good script doesn't automatically spell success. The trick is to be perceptive enough to choose a property that appears to have the best shot at providing entertainment, getting good reviews and making money.

Which brings us to the fourth characteristic—luck! No matter how much money the Producer has managed to raise; no matter how many big named stars are in the show; or how famous the writer or director is, there is only one sure bet, and that is: no bet is a sure thing! Sometimes it just boils down to plain simple luck. Although the Producer's reliance on luck can be minimized by brilliant business decisions, luck will always play a part. It's part of the magic of theatre.

Even though these four characteristics are not essential in order to be "called" a Producer, the ideal and successful Producer will possess these characteristics and more. For our purposes here, we will talk in terms of this *ideal* Producer—even though your mother's beautician may be considering a change in career.

Taking it step by step, let's see what types of things the Producer is involved in during the execution of his job. Keep in mind that this is a simple overview. It is not my intention to describe everything that a Producer does in minute detail. Every show is different and every Producer is different and various attempts at a complete description of the Producer's job and responsibilities have resulted in several books on the subject. Instead I will outline the general overall aspects of the job and hopefully you will get a feel for its scope and dimension.

First of all, the Producer needs to find a show. This is not easy but can happen in a variety of ways. The Producer may get script ideas and suggestions from people he knows or from stars who are looking for starring vehicles for themselves. Writers and composers may pitch their own shows to him and they get this opportunity easily if they are well known. Unknown writers may just take a chance and send their scripts out blindly and unsolicited to Producers and, though very rare, this might actually result in interest and perhaps, if fates are kind and the scripts are good, in Broadway productions.

Shows that were done in the past can be revived by the Producer with a new twist or a new star. There are two or three revivals on Broadway every season. Classic movies have been turned into Broadway shows like: *The Producers, Sweet Smell of Success* and *Mary Poppins.*

Often a Producer will see a small show in some small venue such as Off-Broadway or a Regional theater somewhere and decide that it could make it on Broadway. Seeing a show in production like this gives the Producer a better sense—with audience reactions and lights and sets and costumes—of what the show will be like and how it may be received if it were given an expensive Broadway production.

Let's say, for our purposes here, that our writer and composer, after a long laborious year in front of their computer and piano, were able to turn out the book and score to a musical that they felt sure was terrific and perhaps even successful. And let's say they both worked together on the words to the songs.

Of course, they want to see their labor of love become a show on stage—with actors, scenery, lights and standing ovations from the audience. Along comes our Producer who has his eye on this work and likewise sees great possibilities for it—as a Broadway show. He contacts the writers and they meet and after some discussion decide that they are all willing to take a chance and make the investment in time and money and effort to see if their mutual instincts are correct.

The Option

The first thing that the Producer does is enter into a contract with the writers. This contract is called an "option" and the terms are pretty standard for the most part. The Producer "buys" the "rights" to be the first (or only) Producer of the show, for a cash payment to the writers. The negotiated fee (be it $10,000 or $100,000) buys an option period of six months to a year (sometimes longer) during which time the Producer is guaranteed the exclusive opportunity to produce the show for the stage. Other terms of the option may involve royalties, movie or TV rights (called subsidiary rights), script approval, director/designer considerations, star and/or billing considerations, and so on. The Dramatists Guild (the writer's association) and the musician's Union (American Federation of Musicians) suggests minimum protective guidelines for these contracts and option terms, but the writers and Producer are free to negotiate and make an agreement that suits them over and above the minimums.

Who the writers are, and who the Producer is, can have a great effect on the terms of the option to produce. If we are talking about Producers such as the Shubert Organization, who own half the theaters on Broadway, and a team of unknown writers, then you can bet the Shuberts will be dictating many of the terms and probably paying little money. But if the writers are Broadway veterans, with a proven track record, they will have much more to say not only in terms of the option, but also throughout the ensuing production of their work.

Sometimes an option may freeze a script and nothing happens to it. The writers take this chance because usually a Producer will not pay money for an option on a script that he has no intention of producing. The option can be extended, re-negotiated or renewed while efforts at producing continue. If everything seems on track, the writers stick with the

Producer. If the writers don't feel that the producing effort has been great enough, or that the integrity of their work is being short changed, they may let the option run out and either move on to another Producer or shelve the script all together.

While the option fee itself is guaranteed, actual production of the script is not. For our purposes, however, let's say the show our writer and composer created was optioned for one year and our Producer has every intention of producing the show on Broadway. The writers are content with the arrangement and make themselves available for consultation and possible re-writes. For the next year or longer, the Producer is going to be extremely busy capitalizing the show, finding interested investors, staffing and casting the production, getting the show designed and into rehearsals and planning an opening night party—all this before the option runs out.

Capitalization

After the Producer secures the property in an option, he must raise whatever amount of money will be needed to pay for everything necessary to get the show designed, rehearsed, moved into a theater, and publicized for opening night. Figuring out how much money this will require is called *capitalizing the show*. This initial capital will get the show opened. After that, the Producer will rely on ticket sales to cover weekly operating expenses for as long as the show runs.

These days the production of a musical on Broadway can cost as much as $3,000,000—or more! How does the Producer know how much money he needs? This is where his business experience and knowledge of the theatre comes into play. Based on preliminary discussions with the writers and the production needs outlined in the script, he knows how many professional actors will be needed. The actor's professional Union (Actors' Equity Association) determines actor salaries. If one or more "stars" might be offered contracts, he can pencil in proposed star salaries. He might even approach a few well-known actors with the script and simultaneously begin negotiating with them.

If the Producer has designers in mind to do the sets, lights and costumes, he can have them work up rough preliminary estimates for how much the scenery will cost, how much lighting equipment will be needed and what the wardrobe budget might be. He may have an idea of how many technical stagehands and wardrobe people it will take to build and run the show and the salaries specified by their respective Unions. And from his experience on previous shows, he knows the cost of publicity, theater rentals, scenery construction, lighting equipment rental—and hundreds of other miscellaneous expenses.

With all this planning and discussion, even though most of the figures are estimates and will probably change, the Producer can sit down with his advisors and accountants and come up with a ballpark figure for what their financial requirements will be to produce the show. And they will usually overestimate just to be on the safe side.

When a Producer is seeking money from sources outside his own office or circle of friends, the law requires that a projected budget be furnished to all prospective investors. Investors can then purchase percentages of the show (called points) for certain amounts of money hoping to get a return on their investment if the show is a hit. The cost of each point is usually based on selling a minimum of 50% of the show at a price that will produce the required capitalization. The remaining 50% of the show is retained by the Producer or negotiated away to stars, directors or designers in lieu of large salaries.

Let's say that our show has been capitalized at $2,000,000. Then, in simple terms, 1 point (or 1% of the show) would cost an investor $40,000, so that 50% or 50 points multiplied by $40,000 equals the required $2,000,000 capitalization. If a Producer is having trouble selling the show, he may elect to give away some of his own points to attract investors. Thus an investor may receive 2, 3 or 4 points for the same $40,000 investment. This is common practice and perfectly legal as long as the Producer doesn't dispose of more than 100% of the show which would be a problem when percentages of profits were to be paid back.

Only a misguided Producer would attempt to produce a Broadway musical without raising enough money or by overselling the show to investors. This conundrum is the basis for the Broadway hit *The Producers.*

Finding Investors

Since our Producer knows what he is doing, he sets out to find the necessary investors and raise the necessary capital so that his production is adequately funded and has every opportunity to succeed. He can do this in one of three ways: he can either put up all the money himself (like Rosie O'Donnell did in the Fall of 2003 for her Broadway show *Taboo* staring Boy George); he can invite investors who have previously invested in any of his or other shows to invest again; or he can mount what is known as a "workshop production" or "backer's audition" to interest potential backers.

Obviously, if our Producer puts up all the money himself then, aside from necessarily being very rich, he retains all the points on the show and will receive all the profits if the show is a success. Very few individuals can do this. Broadway Producers such as the Shuberts, Nederlanders, the Jujamcyns or Disney are more suited and able to produce with their own money.

If the Producer is reaching out to others then logically he will start with people he knows, who have money, and who may have invested in Broadway in the past. Not all investment opportunities on Broadway result in profits, but there are people who can and do invest repeatedly in the hopes that there will be a big pay off down the road.

A "backer's audition" can be an intimate presentation by the composer of the musical score with the writer telling the story. This presentation can take place in someone's home or in a hotel room or in a studio or even a theatre that has been rented for a day. All it requires is a piano. A larger "workshop" presentation may be a mini version of the show including some cast members, maybe a potential star and maybe even some costumes and props and limited scenery. This presentation would likely take place in a theater. Either way, the point of these presentations is to audition the show in front of potential backers so they can actually see and hear what the show is about and theoretically be more inclined to open their wallets with some money to invest.

When potential investors show an interest and offer their money, our Producer will enter into *limited partnership agreements* with them and deposits their money in the company bank account. When enough capital is raised, it's full steam ahead.

Production Staff

After the necessary capital has been secured and all of the limited partnership agreements have been signed, the Producer must hire the business and artistic staff for the show. Producers who produce on a regular basis in New York have offices and in-house production staffs already in place. In some instances, like with the aforementioned Shuberts, Nederlanders, Jujamcyns and Disney, the production staff may already be operating currently running Broadway shows.

First, the Producer will designate his right hand man, called the general manager, who is, in all likelihood, a permanent member of the Producer's production team.

Together they will handle every arrangement and business deal concerning the show. As the Producer's right hand, the general manager acts on behalf of the Producer and carries the same authority as the Producer when dealing with the show's business. The Producer can, and many times does, act as his own general manager. The intelligent Producer hires the best general manager that he can find—presumably someone who possesses the same astute knowledge of business and of theatre. A show without a competent general manager already has one strike against it.

Artistically, the most important person that the Producer hires is the director. He may even come aboard during capitalization so that he can help visualize the show's possibilities and advise the Producer on casting and design needs. Some Producers use the same directors again and again because they know and trust their work. "Trying out" a new director on a Broadway show is very rare, although, if a Producer has optioned a property that is currently "in development" then the property may come with its own director. This may also occur if a show moves from a smaller venue such as Off-Broadway to a full Broadway production. At any rate, the Producer must have complete confidence in his director because the real artistic success of the show is the director's domain.

The designers are hired when they are needed, most assuredly prior to the beginning of rehearsals, so that the director knows what his "environment" will look like as he begins his work. Often designers come on board as early as the capitalization process because there are "star" designers who, by virtue of the fact that they are on the project, can help sell the show to investors. Designers can also help the Producer develop the budget for the show. Design responsibilities, as mentioned, are pretty self-explanatory—sets, props, lights and costumes. There will also probably be a sound designer for our musical, and a hair and makeup designer, and depending on the show, possibly a special effects designer. Many times one designer may design more than one aspect of the show.

If the show is a musical, a choreographer will be hired. Or, if you can get Susan Stroman, you will have a director *and* choreographer all rolled into one! The choreographer is responsible for all of the musically accompanied movement onstage. Sometimes this is actual dancing; sometimes this is only fluid, musically accompanied crowd control.

The production stage manager comes on board next. The PSM may have worked for the Producer or the director before. He is the director's right hand man and sees to it that the director's needs and desires are met in terms of what goes on the stage. Among these four people—the Producer, general manager, director and stage manager—every decision concerning our show is made. (More on these people in subsequent chapters.)

A company manager is hired if she isn't already a member of the Producer's team. This person handles all the details pertaining directly to members of the company— contracts, paychecks, per diems, perks, plane tickets, show tickets, hotels, house seats etc.

Then, a myriad of others: a production office staff, associates and assistants to almost everyone, legal people, publicity people, casting people and accounting people. Then, like a snowball down a mountain, the show that started as an idea takes on a life of its own as a fully formed business.

The Producer has booked an available theater. Since he must rent the theater for a specific time, he has probably decided on an opening night. If the Producer and director have hired one or more stars, which usually happens early in the process—even early enough to help "sell" the show to prospective backers—a press agent may begin to put out some advance publicity in an effort to generate some excitement for the show. General casting notices have gone out and auditions are scheduled. Agents have been contacted for casting ideas. The orchestration of the score is underway and a musical director/conductor is hired. An orchestra contractor is lined up to put together the orchestra from members of the Musician's Union (in New York it's AFM Local #802). Union bonds are posted to guarantee salary payments.

As soon as the set, lights and costume designs have been approved then a production supervisor is hired as well as a carpenter, electrician, prop person, wardrobe supervisor and sound operator. Appropriate shops are contracted to build or provide the scenic elements and to create the costumes.

From idea, through capitalization, to staffing, the Producer and members of his team may have already invested six months of time. And there may be another six months or year to go before opening night. There are hundreds of details, obligations, deadlines, purchases, contracts and arrangements that the Producer will deal with and, if he doesn't handle them directly, they are taken care of by the general manager or the company manager or the production stage manager or even the lawyers. It is a full time business with office hours extending well beyond 9-5.

Into Production

Once the cast has been auditioned and hired and everyone is signed to a contract, the rehearsals begin. The early rehearsals usually take place in a rehearsal studio. The Producer will attend, occasionally, as will the writers, but this is the director's domain and this is where the show begins to take shape.

The shops are building the scenery and putting together the lighting equipment. The cast has fittings and the costumes are being made.

Additional money may be needed, sought and

secured. There is insurance (property, injury & casualty) and the theater license to sign (guaranteeing the use of the theater). There are salaries and a multitude of incidental expenses. There are meetings with accountants and attorneys and Unions and agents. There are problems and mistakes and injuries and delays. Decisions, decisions, decisions. Everything is crucial. Everyone wants to talk to the Producer—all the time. Everything must be decided—now! In short, the Producer's job is everything.

After the opening night party, and if the show is a hit, the pressure and number of decisions may begin to taper off a bit. Things will settle down to the paying of the bills each week including salaries and rent and operating expenses (called "the nut"), and maintaining publicity in order to keep the show open so that those bills can be paid.

The press agent is constantly "selling" the show. Some technical elements may need repair or replacement. A new cast member or two may be needed. If the show runs long, anniversary parties are planned. Everything is the Producers business. It's a big job and a tremendous responsibility and it doesn't end until long after the show closes and all the bills are paid and all the accounts are closed and all the investors are either paid back or sent a letter of regrets and thanks.

Then it all starts all over again when the Producer finds another show.

I have never produced a Broadway show. But I have worked with several Producers and production teams. I have seen the range of talent from best to worst. I have been honored to work with some of the best Producers on Broadway, and I have regretted the times I ever took jobs from the worst—no matter how much they paid me. But I have learned from everything. When I produced several modern dance concerts in the late 80s, I incorporated the knowledge I had acquired and tried to follow the good examples that were set. And I can tell you—being a Producer isn't an easy job!

I was being a bit facetious at the beginning of this chapter when I suggested that *anyone* could be a Producer. While it is true that you can stick a label on anyone, only a small handful of those professionals who are labeled Producer can actually handle the job.

Scene 3 : THE DIRECTOR

The Director is unquestionably the most important artistic person that the producer hires. It is through the Director's overall vision and leadership that a script grows from the printed page to a living performance. A good Director can take a bad or risky script and mold it into a work of art. A bad Director can take a brilliant script and turn it into a piece of garbage. Certainly there are unavoidable factors and unforeseen circumstances that may affect the success of a show. In general, however, it is the Director who guides and shapes all of the human, technical and artistic elements, thereby taking on the responsibility for ultimate success or failure of the show.

The Director is the primary interpreter, the visionary and the inspiration. He is the master artist, and with his palette of colors (actors), his canvas (the stage), and his inspiration (the script), he paints the picture for the audience to see, hear, feel and perhaps even remember—long after they have left the theater.

In the last section we described the producer as the big boss, the top banana. If this is true, how then can the Director be the one in charge, with the overall vision? Are there two bosses?

In a sense—yes. And it can sometimes be a very precarious relationship. The Director, by tradition, and in every professional sense, is the leader of the show. His ideas, methods and interpretations are the root of the show's form and structure. He is the painter, as we have said. But the producer paid for the canvas and the colors, and so the Director is held accountable by the producer for everything that he does. The Director is the artist but the producer pays the bills. If business isn't going too well, no matter how inspired the Director might be, the Director either changes direction or the producer changes the Director.

How can this potential trauma be avoided? After all, it is rare that two people will think exactly the same way about every aspect of a multi-million dollar Broadway musical. And no one really wants to upset the apple cart by changing a leader right in the middle of the campaign. What can be done to avoid such a disaster?

First of all, it would be wise to hire a good Director. When the producer is considering prospective Directors, there should be intensive discussions about ideas, intentions and approaches to the show. The producer also takes into consideration his own personal knowledge of the Director based on a previous relationship or reputation. With all this information, the producer can usually select a Director that he can work *with* rather than *against*. It only makes good business sense.

On my first Broadway show as a stage manager, the producer wanted complete and total control over everything—including the artistic elements. So he hired a Director who agreed to do what he was told and who wasn't permitted his own artistic vision. This was a fairly new Director who agreed to the arrangement in order to get the Broadway credit. Needless to say the show went into production with many problems and too many people making bad decisions resulting in general chaos to the point of anarchy. The show got terrible reviews and closed almost immediately. In general you could write a book about this adventure titled: "How NOT to do a Broadway Show." (I may refer to this disaster throughout this book because I have learned many things from this major mistake.)

The Producer / Director relationship is very special, and it is the wise producer who respects the domain of the Director. Likewise, it is the professional Director who will consider the producer's suggestions and criticisms. After all, they both want the same thing—success. As Shakespeare said, "The play's the thing."

Even if the producer and the Director are friends, a contract is signed when the Director is hired. On Broadway, this contract is administered by The Society of Stage Directors and Choreographers (S.S.D.&C). The S.S.D.&C. establishes minimum salary requirements and monitors certain conditions that protect the Director while he is employed, including salary, royalties and billing.

The Director, in most professional situations, gets paid a fee for his services. The fee can be negotiated, like any salary, and is based on the Director's background and level of previous success. There are "star" Directors just like there are "star" actors. The fee can be paid on a weekly basis, or sometimes it is broken down into three payments coming due at the beginning of rehearsals, the middle of rehearsals and finally on opening night. The Director can also negotiate a royalty, which is paid weekly as long as the show remains open. This royalty acknowledges that, even after opening night, when the Director's direct involvement is limited, his work remains on view until the show closes.

No easy task

The Director's function, simply stated, is to bridge the gap between the script and the audience, via the performers. Following the story and character guidelines set down by the writers, and under the budgetary constraints defined by the producer regarding scenery, props and costumes, the Director must create an atmosphere where the words of the writer's story will live. Under his supervision friends will meet, and enemies or lovers, relationships will blossom, feelings will be revealed, and he will guide the dramatic twists and turns in order to affect the audience in such a way that they not only hear the words being spoken, but understand the feelings and meanings behind them. The blending of the words and music with the talents of the performers, within the technical and scenic environment given him, is no easy task.

You can go to school and follow a curriculum that is geared to being a Director; you can be a frustrated actor always thinking you know how to do it better; you can be a writer who never was satisfied by the way others interpreted your work; or, you can have a lot of money and just decide one day you'd like to direct a show. Directors come from everywhere. Some of them are gifted and inspired enough to succeed. Others are not. Talent is the difference.

Pre-production

Usually, before every member of the staff is hired or the cast is chosen, the Director can spend weeks engaged in lengthy discussions with the writer and composer regarding the story, characters, relationships, emotions, intentions and meaning of the script and score. It is the writer's work that the Director must translate to the stage and, therefore, the Director must understand it thoroughly. Because the script inspires every facet of the show, the Director immerses himself in the world that was created for him. The story is broken down in terms of dramatic content as well as dramatic action. Characters are interpreted based on their significance to the story and their relationships to each other. Dialogue is analyzed and, in many cases, adapted by the writer. The music is analyzed for its emotional and dramatic effect. Through all of this it could be said that the Director figuratively becomes one of the writers, and it is rather commonly accepted that a script will undergo many changes due to a Director's input before rehearsals begin six months or a year later.

After the design team has been assembled, the Director and designers discuss the Director's vision for the show. Later, when the scenery, lighting and costume designs are submitted for approval, the Director must be able to determine if they correspond to his artistic vision—and the writer's intentions. There is much to be considered and very often many problems will need to be worked out. Do the scenic elements enhance the show or will they detract from it? Have all the doors, windows, tables and chairs that are needed for the action of the script been included? Will the lighting create the proper mood or effect? (Sometimes this may not be known until the lights are actually hung in the theater and turned on.) Are the costumes appropriate and functional or will they be cumbersome and unsuitable? Will everything be interesting and compliment the work of the actors or will the scenic elements over-power the human elements and get in the way—or even be dangerous?

It is important that these questions and dozens more be answered before plans are finalized and money is spent—in order to avoid costly alterations later. It would be a disaster if hundreds of thousands of dollars were spent on technical and scenic elements that arrived at the theater in six months—and they were all wrong in relation to the Director's vision. Hence, it is essential that the Director understand the work of the designers in order to be able to communicate with them. It is the rare Director who will say to a designer, "Do what you want." And it is the professional Director who will respect the efforts and craft of the designers and work cooperatively toward their mutual goal.

Casting

Many times, these days, a Broadway show is put together as a "package." This means that there are elements to a particular show that are arranged and put in place before the show gets off the ground, through capitalization and into rehearsals. Some usual elements of a package may include popular writers and/or composers, a well-known Director and one or more stars—all of whom, by their very involvement in the project, can help to generate interest, investment and hopefully success.

Disney's *The Lion King* is an example of a package where the Broadway version of the movie came complete with Sir Elton John and Tim Rice as composers and Julie Taymor was added as the Director. Although this show didn't need to find investors because Disney produced it, the show was advertised with heavy emphasis on these "star" names. *Bells Are Ringing,* a 2001 revival of the 50s Comden and Green hit, was packaged with popular Broadway star Faith Prince signed on to play the Billie Holliday role and a relative unknown director, Tina Landau. *The Lion King* was a big hit. *Bells Are Ringing* was not. (I worked as a stagehand on both shows.)

If shows are packaged as star vehicles, then these stars may be hired by the producer even before the Director is hired and, although the Director will usually go along with the choice, he may not have been consulted in this casting choice. But in all other casting consideration, it is the Director who makes the choices.

Producers, writers, stars, choreographers, musical directors and even stage managers, may contribute suggestions or be asked to voice their opinions about casting, but the Director usually has the final word. Only the Director has the complete vision of the show in his mind: how he sees the characters and the style of the show. The Director will consider many things as he puts together the company of actors that will fit his over all vision.

Actors are *usually* chosen for their acting talent. If, however, there is a lot of dancing in the show, casting decisions are based on dance ability. Similarly for a show that is built around a score, singers are given some preference. Very often, however, performers are chosen for intangible reasons as well—like a "look" or a "body type."

During the audition process, which could take weeks or even
months, the Director evaluates the talent with regard to the
needs of the script. He plays different actors against each
other, samples their singing and dancing abilities and looks
to find the perfect mix and match of performers who will
bring the script and score to life.

To see and judge this talent, the Director must have
talent himself. And so it is very rare to find a professional
Director (especially on Broadway) who has not acted at
some point in his career.

Rehearsals

This is where the work gets done. For the actors and
the Director, the rehearsal process is the meat of their lives.
Some have called it a grind. Most come alive during this
diligent, deliberate, exhaustive creative period.

During the rehearsal process, the Director is literally
a chameleon, changing constantly as each artistic—and not
so artistic—need arises. Not only is the Director the
inspirational force who pampers, demands and shapes
performances on stage, but also, often times, his inspiration
extends off-stage as well. At various times, with various
people, he is a friend or a teacher; a drill sergeant or a priest;
a psychiatrist, a mother or a brother. He is every inspiration,
quiet or loud, serious or humorous, that is necessary to make
the working environment a creative one with as little stress
as possible. The work must get done—the dialogue must be
memorized, the choreography must be learned the songs
must find their voices—and it is the Director's responsibility
to see to it that all is accomplished according to his artistic
vision and the production timetable.

Step by step, day by day, element by element, the
Director shapes and molds his vision. He determines the
movement of the actors on the stage (called "blocking"). He
draws out of them interpretations of their roles and their

relationships that blend with the other characters. He makes sure the words are spoken with the same meaning that the writer intended—and loud enough for the last row of the balcony to hear. He melds what the choreographer gives him in movement into, around and through each scene. He mixes the voices and blends them with the musical director into the dramatic sound that is required. He sees to it that the scenic elements are unified and work fluidly within the context of the vision; that the stage settings become the environment; that the lighting creates the proper mood; and that the costumes make us believe who the actors really are.

The Director inspires and changes and fixes and polishes and unifies the show into a cohesive whole. He paints the picture with his colors and brushes and, after all of the rehearsals and all of the work, he hangs the finished product up for the audience to see. He is, as was said at the outset, the most important artistic person that the producer hires.

I directed a few shows while I was in college. It was after I had acted in a couple of dozen shows and worked backstage on several others and I wanted to stretch myself.

For my first adventure, I wanted to do a show that had a special meaning for me. I chose Robert Anderson's *I Never Sang for My Father.* It was a challenge for us all, especially the two student actors in my cast who portrayed people who were older than themselves. We had a great time. The audiences seemed to like the production and I even won an Outstanding Director Award presented by the faculty of the Theatre Department.

The following year I directed a fun show to do— *Butterflies Are Free* written by Leonard Gershe and made into a movie in 1972 starring Goldie Hawn. Next I was hired to direct a production of Neil Simon's *The Odd Couple* for a Canton, Ohio High School. And finally, during my last semester, I directed the play I wrote about Abraham Lincoln, followed by my Master's thesis directing project—a play called *Low on High.*

Although my directing experiences don't compare in scope to Broadway, I took my job seriously, dealt with all the same elements, was challenged by the same problems and pitfalls and endeavored to create a finished product that an audience might cherish. I chose the scripts and analyzed them (without the benefit of the authors—except for Burton Russell on *Low On High*), made the casting decisions, worked out technical details and artistic choices with my designers, organized the rehearsal schedule and put the cast through their paces as we created our shows. So I, like any Director, was responsible for what the end result was—good or bad.

Having held other positions on different shows helped me to be a better Director—especially having been an actor. Directing, in turn, has broadened my awareness of what it takes, and how difficult it is, to mount a large scale production.

Would I ever direct again? I think I would. Perhaps something Off-Broadway or as a guest Director in a college somewhere. I had a good time when I directed. The results were more than satisfactory. I didn't, however, continue a career as a Director because it was never a goal and even though I might have had a future in directing, my career took several other paths instead.

After Opening Night

What happens to the Director after a show opens—after all the hard work, frustration, challenges, changes, sleepless nights, and long stressful days—after the applause and the reviews?

Well, if the show is a hit and runs for any length of time, the Director may return from time to time to watch the show and tighten up some things that may be getting loose. This would most certainly happen if a new star were going into the show. In fact, most contracts specifically require the Director's presence at these special times. Eventually the Director disappears and is rarely seen except for anniversary parties.

A Director may be involved with mounting any National Tours of the show, which wouldn't get underway for a year or more. (More on National Tours later.)

If the show is a flop, the Director, like everyone else, heads for the unemployment office. Or, if lucky or successful, the Director will move on to the next show. If the Director has a hit on the boards then chances are he will have another show in no time. A flop means the next producer will ask more questions. There is a saying: "You're only as good as your last job."

The Choreographer

The Choreographer is also a Director.   Sometimes they are one and the same person, as in *The Producers* and *Young Frankenstein*—Directed *and* Choreographed by Susan Stroman. But just as designers generally only design one aspect of a show, so too, Directors and Choreographers try to divide up the responsibilities.

Obviously,   the   Choreographer   is   singularly responsible for the movement of the performers on the stage. If the show has a musical number with dancing and singing, the show has a Choreographer. In the big splashy musicals such as *42nd Street,* the Choreographer is responsible for all of the big dance numbers. She will also stage the other moments of the show where the performers are moving onstage but not dancing. For instance, the transitions between each scene sometimes require performers to move props or scenery to effect a smooth transition. The Choreographer is shaping this movement, primarily to keep it organized, safe, and efficient, but also to keep it within the style of the show.

The collaboration between the Director and the Choreographer is a unique one. The Director is in charge, but he will generally not step on the Choreographer's toes regarding the musical numbers. They have surely worked things out between them in terms of the style of the show and so they each deal with their own area somewhat independently. While the Director deals with the book scenes and character development, the Choreographer is shaping the dancing. The Director will make sure the dances flow out of the scenes, not just in terms of movement, but also in terms of character and mood. And since singing and dancing take the place of dialogue and blocking, they must also be believable as part of the whole show.

Choreographers are most often former dancers who have spent years training. Many of them have performed as dancers in other Broadway shows earlier in their careers— for other Choreographers. Not all dancers go on to become Choreographers. Not all Choreographers are successful.

Musical Director

The Musical Director directs all things pertaining to the score, the singing, the lyrics and the orchestra. He makes sure the score is sung correctly and all the lyrics can be heard and understood. He may have worked with the composer to develop the orchestrations. He will help decide what instruments are needed in the orchestra. He will collaborate with the orchestra contractor to hire the orchestra.

The Musical Director is responsible for the overall musical sound of the show. He will oversee all rehearsals, teach all music to the actors and, along with the Director shape and mold the musical performances of the actors toward the desired goal.

Very often the Musical Director will stay with the show and conduct the orchestra during performances as well as run musical rehearsals and replacement put-ins.

Scene 4 : THE STAGE MANAGER

Taking every job and every position into consideration—from beginning to end—from before auditions until after closing night, the position of Stage Manager is probably the most unique and critical position that exists in the theatre. Because of this immense responsibility there is never only one Stage Manager on an individual show. The minimum number is two and, with some larger musicals, there can be as many as five Stage Managers—headed by a Production Stage Manager (PSM). Each Stage Managerial team handles all the production responsibilities of a particular show, in a fluid and unique way, depending on the people involved on the team. Individual responsibilities are delegated according to the working relationship of the team. The only consistent factor from one Stage Managerial team to the next is that the PSM is the on site "go to" person with final say about everything regarding the nightly running of the show in the theater.

Stage Managers are of either sex and come in all ages, shapes and sizes, hired for any of a variety of reasons. In the past, assistants were hired because they could act and therefore were used as understudies. So too, a dance captain, whose job it is to maintain the choreography, might also have performed some of the duties of an Assistant Stage Manager. These practices are pretty much obsolete now. On Broadway, Stage Managers generally do not perform any other function.

Often times a PSM may hire a spouse or paramour as an assistant. I have seen this practice work exceedingly well.

And I have also seen this practice fail miserably. The best teams are made up of people who complement each other and who have strong individual characteristics and backgrounds. On one team there might be an assistant who was strong with paperwork and another who had a background in the technical aspects of theatre. Or there might be an assistant who can handle the egos of the performers—stroking them and making them happy and satisfied. If the PSM wants a smooth running show, he or she will first put together a smooth running Stage Managerial team.

I was a Stage Manager early in my career. My strong suit was my technical background. I had assistants who took up the slack in other areas. Or I worked as an assistant to others who would rely on my technical background. I got jobs because I was a male . . . and I lost jobs for the same reason—because there was a need for a female on the team for balance. I once lost a Broadway Assistant Stage Manager job because I would have had to understudy one of the roles and the casting director decided I wasn't "right" for the part.

While the Stage Managerial team may posses differing talents or areas of expertise, they all must (and generally do) possess organizational skills and leadership qualities and, in general, they really need to have a pleasant personality. In short . . . the team really has to know what is going on at all times with every aspect of the show, and they need to communicate with and get along with everyone who works on the show.

The Hub of the Wheel

The PSM and his team can best be described as the hub of the wheel. Not that the wheel (the show) revolves around the Stage Managers, but rather that the Stage Managers are always, and necessarily, at the center of everything that concerns the show and must make sure everything is well greased and rolls along smoothly. All information regarding cast, crew and staff is funneled through the Stage Managers. All scheduling information pertaining to any aspect of the show is cleared through the Stage Managers. The Stage Managers are alerted to all decisions made by directors, choreographers, musical directors, designers and the producer's office that have any bearing on the show. The Stage Managers are usually the first people in the rehearsal hall or theater and almost always the last people to leave.

The best Stage Managers, like the best directors, have an understanding and working knowledge of all aspects of the theatre. The Production Stage Manager is the only member of the staff that is in constant contact with every other member of the staff from the producer, general manager and director, to designers and crew, to actors, house manager and press agents.

Pre-production

The PSM is probably already at work even before rehearsals begin and maybe even before any assistants are hired. He is usually included in all preliminary discussions concerning the script, scenic elements and casting, and often times is called upon to offer helpful objective suggestions in each of these areas.

He will begin to generate notes and paperwork that deal with the multitude of show elements as they are discussed, formulated, changed and decided. The script requirements that are related to casting needs and scenic, lighting and prop details are enumerated. All information is logged into a Production Book which will become the ultimate reference book for information on the show.

He assists the producer in organizing casting interviews and auditions including the rental of studio and theater space. He may arrange for transportation to and from casting meetings for the staff as well as for actors, depending upon their notoriety. He will conduct smooth running auditions by keeping the process moving and maintaining efficient use of time. He will organize and maintain all comments and notes regarding individual actors for future reference. He may even arrange for coffee or other meals during staff meetings and auditions.

He will collaborate with the general manager on a production schedule including dates, place and time of rehearsals and the implementation of technical elements. He will be in constant contact with and relay information between the director, the writer, the composer, the musical director, the choreographer and the designers. He will monitor the progress of the construction of the scenic elements, and the gathering of props. He will provide access to the press agents for the show and help arrange for meetings with any stars to begin formulating a publicity campaign. He may even facilitate a photo shoot involving show stars so that some pre-publicity can begin to be generated and a show poster and theater marquee can be designed.

On Broadway, the PSM has become so important and vital to the production that he may have billing on the show posters.

Rehearsals

Usually by the time auditions commence and definitely by the time rehearsals begin the Production Stage Manager has selected his assistants—even though he doesn't actually hire them or pay them. They are generally people with whom he has worked in the past and feels comfortable with as team players. A producer may have some suggestions for assistants, and, like it or not, may impose these decisions on the PSM. (I once lost a Broadway Assistant Stage Manager position to a Producer's office assistant.) This will happen usually when the PSM has limited experience and may in fact ask the producer for suggestions. Generally the PSM makes the choices because the PSM has to do the job and he needs a team that he can rely on to help handle the myriad of responsibilities.

During rehearsals, the Production Stage Manager is the director's right hand. He is ever present at the director's side and privy to all conversations regarding the show. He will keep notes for the director regarding the action on the stage—taking constant notes on blocking, scenery shifts and lighting, sound and prop cues. He will offer suggestions, help solve problems and help work out conflicts. Nothing happens during rehearsals that the PSM doesn't know about.

Early rehearsals usually take place in rehearsal studios because there is no need to be on the stage paying for a theatre rental and crew to be present in the early stages of rehearsals. In the rehearsal studio the Stage Managers will put colored tape on the floor to designate the size and shape of the stage set and the placement of essential pieces of scenery. This helps the actors get a sense of spacing as they begin to start working out the scenes. The PSM will furnish the production prop person with a list of props to be used in the show. These actual props or their facsimile will be collected and available in the rehearsal studio so that the actors can use them and get used to them as soon as possible.

While the PSM is spending time with the director and handling the major issues, his team is busy with a multitude of other details—all accomplished with the awareness, guidance and direction of the PSM. They formulate and maintain the elaborate production schedule involving all elements of the show, and keep everyone informed of any changes. They coordinate with the wardrobe department to schedule costume fittings for all the actors and keep track of every costume change that may occur throughout the show. They facilitate script changes with updated pages on a daily basis. They schedule actors to meet publicity engagements with the press agent.

In the event that dance rehearsals or vocal rehearsals are in separate rooms or separate buildings or at different times, a Stage Manager will be in each place or maintain contact with the choreographer and musical director and keep the director informed of these activities.

Tech Rehearsals

When the cast moves to the theater, the show goes into technical rehearsals, and all of the technical elements begin to be added. The Assistant Stage Managers take positions on the stage to make sure everything runs smoothly, efficiently and safely. And they keep notes concerning prop placement and movement, scenery shifts, costume changes and the overall pattern of the general backstage operation of the show.

Meantime, out in the audience, an elaborate array of tables has been arranged over the theater seats to accommodate the production staff. The lighting department usually has the most tables with computers and other equipment to control the lights during rehearsals. The lighting designer is there with various assistants and lighting board operators. The set designer, the costume designer, the director and the Production Stage Manager all have separate tables from which they conduct their business during the rehearsal process. The PSM is always near the director and close to the designers and monitors all communication between them as they light the show and work out scenery and costume changes. The PSM makes notes of all actor entrances, scenery moves, lighting cues and sound cues in his master production script.

Just as the director is responsible for everything that happens onstage in view of the audience, so too the Production Stage Manager and his assistants are responsible for everything that happens backstage—out of the audiences' view. They make sure that the actors make their entrances from the right places at the right times and all of the props are available. They cue the light changes over a headset, and cue the stagehands moving the scenery by blinking a stage cue light. They monitor noise and safety. They supervise every backstage detail that is happening and that must be accomplished. The Stage Managers are constantly working and always busy—paying attention to what is going on and taking notes concerning trouble spots.

Running the Show

After the show opens and the director leaves to direct his next show, the Production Stage Manager is responsible for the maintenance of the show. He gives performance notes to the actors and stagehands. He conducts brush-up rehearsals. He assists in cast replacement and rehearses new cast members who join the show after opening night.

He will help arrange house seat orders for the company members and schedule vacation time. Safety issues are constantly checked. The condition of the wardrobe and scenery and props are monitored and work calls are scheduled when necessary. He will keep a journal of every detail of the day-to-day operation of the show and issue daily Stage Manager Reports so that the producer's office can keep track of what is going on in the theater.

Sometimes it seems that the work of the Stage Manager is never done—in fact sometimes some Stage Managers actually do some paper work at home in order to just keep up with keeping track of all the elements of the show. In general, the Production Stage Manager and his team have the responsibility of making sure that the show is as fresh and as wonderful for each new audience as it was for the first audience on opening night—no matter how long the show runs.

The Stage Managerial team compiles all the

information concerning the production and running of the show into the master Production Book which will include the final version of the script; scenery, light, sound and costume plots; equipment inventory and prop lists; and scenery shifts and acting notes. Many times, especially with a new show, this production book may become the actual published version of the show.

After Closing Night

After the show closes (with any luck, not for a few years), the Production Stage Manager and his assistants are involved with the breakdown and load-out of the show from the theater. They work together with the show's electrician, carpenter and prop person to make sure that any rented or borrowed equipment is returned to the appropriate vendor, that any scenery and/or costumes are sent to storage if they are being saved.

The team will dismantle the Stage Manager's office in the theater and put together all pertinent information on the show which will be stored in a warehouse or in the producer's office—if one will continue to exist. They will make sure that the company contact sheet is printed for everyone so those company members who choose to stay in touch can do so.

All of this breakdown can take as little as a week or two, and as much as a month, depending on the size of the show. And then, the Stage Managers move on to their next gig.

The Production Stage Manager and his assistants, like all of the actors, must be members of Actors' Equity Association which is the labor Union that protects all actors (including dancers and singers) and Stage Managers. Stage Managers have always been included in the performers' Union based on the past practice of using an Assistant Stage Manager as an understudy on a show. Despite the fact that now-a-days this practice rarely occurs Stage Managers are still members of the performers' Union because there is no other more appropriate Union.

Now it should be fairly obvious how the Stage Managers are the hub of the wheel at the center of the ongoing operation of a show. Quite frankly, it is impossible to detail the scope of responsibilities and duties that are performed by the Stage Managerial team. It is not unrealistic to state that there are countless details and courtesies that each Stage Manager addresses before, during and after the production of a show, which may go unspecified, undisclosed and usually unnoticed—but that are all intrinsic to the show's smooth, effortless, professional operation.

The Stage Managers must have a broad background of knowledge and must be competent in a wide variety of abilities from taking notes, to directing, to smoothing flustered egos. It is difficult to overestimate the magnitude of responsibility inherent in the position of the Stage Manager, and hence, the vital significance of the people who can execute the function of the Stage Manager position with sufficient versatility, proficiency, organization and good humor.

The times I worked as a Stage Manager were some of the most challenging yet satisfying times in my career. I would have continued on in this area except for two reasons: there were too few jobs available with too many other people competing for them, and I began working as a stagehand which turned out to be a busy and lucrative career path.

In the early 80's I helped launch the Stage Managers' Association (http://www.stagemanagers.org/) to help young stage managers meet and network with working and established stage managers, and share information and ideas. I still keep in touch with many of my stage manager friends.

Scene 5 : THE DESIGNERS

In general, for every show, there are three visual elements that must be designed: the scenery, the lighting and the costumes. These three elements help to create the overall environment where the play or musical takes place. Scenery for a show can range from a bare stage with one or more changeable backdrops and a few props; to a simple living room box set; to elaborate multi-set environments that are almost constantly changing and become part of the show itself. Lighting, as well, can be simple or extravagant. And depending upon the nature of the show, the costumes can either be modern day clothes easily purchased, or elaborate period attire that requires time and money to find, create and maintain.

Just because there are three visual elements does not mean there have to be three Designers. Very often a set Designer may also design the costumes. On rare occasions, one Designer may design everything. Shows with small budgets try to streamline the scenic elements and one way to do this is by hiring fewer Designers. Conversely, sometimes the scenic elements are so overdone that they overshadow the actors and may even get better reviews.

Producers (especially on Broadway) hire Designers based on background, proven expertise and even preliminary design suggestions. Producers may have a certain group of Designers that they frequently work with because they are familiar with and trusting of their work. Scenery, lighting and costumes can be the costliest upfront aspects of a show and if a producer is unfamiliar with a Designer's work there could be disastrous results.

I once worked on a small Off-Broadway show that required two completely different sets which would be changed at intermission. Each finished set looked great and the director loved them. But to change from one set to another required a large stage crew and more time than the length of a customary intermission. The Designer failed to take this into consideration and kept telling everyone that everything would be fine. Also, because of budget constraints, the sets were built so inexpensively that they began to fall apart each time they were moved. After the first week of the show, portions of the set were in need of repair, hence more money spent. The Set Designer meant well, but he failed the reality test. Even though a smarter Broadway producer may have seen this coming, it is doubtful that this Designer made the leap to the big league unless he came to his senses.

Failure of design, however, is not always the fault of a Designer. On my first Broadway show I watched wonderful costume designs being cut down and oversimplified by a producer who hadn't raised enough capital for his show. He had to cut corners and the result was a hodge-podge of costumes thrown together, rented, borrowed or bought, that had to be fixed daily at mounting extra costs. The upkeep expenses finally doubled the original budget. In this case I'm sure the Costume Designer took great pains to avoid this producer in the future.

For our purposes, we will concern ourselves with three Designers and their efficient professional work on Broadway. From this discussion one can generalize to fit other design and theatrical situations as well as get an idea of how much can go wrong in this costly area of the business.

The Scenic Designer

The Scenic Designer is a very unique artist who works on paper and in model-making as well as in full three dimensions. The Scenic Designer's unique form of artistry is one of translation, imagination and re-creation. It is the Scenic Designer's job to translate the needs of the script and the desires of the director, using his imagination and the specific tools of his trade, into an environment that can be re-created on stage—within the budget.

To be able to bring to life this environment onstage requires more than just an imaginative idea or the knack for rendering interesting drawings. Re-creating a design in three-dimensional form requires some specialized practical abilities. More than likely the Scenic Designer is a competent draftsman, an experienced carpenter and a knowledgeable engineer all rolled into one. Most Designers may have learned or perfected their skills in school. But to really learn the craft, chances are they spent many years as a carpenter reading the drawings and building the sets of other Designers. Not all carpenters become Designers, but nearly all Designers have worked in shops learning to understand the skills they will need.

Becoming a Scenic Designer is prompted by an interest in theatre and a talent for visualizing, drawing and creating, and by a desire to see imagination become reality. For all practical purposes, the Scenic Designer takes the construction of a set into account even as it is being designed. In many instances the building of a typical box set is similar to the construction of a house, or at least various rooms of a house, with walls and windows and doors and floors. Although the methods and materials are adapted and scaled down somewhat for the stage, the principles and the desired visual effect are the same. And since no one wants an onstage wall to fall down and hurt someone, it is vital that specific safe construction techniques are known and followed.

These days the main structure of most Broadway sets is constructed out of steel and/or aluminum. This framework is covered in treated plywood and Masonite on the deck or floor, and by other materials such as fabric, plexi-glass, fiberglass or even Styrofoam on the walls. Painted backdrops are made of muslin. Curtains are made from velour or loosely woven scrim material. Everything on a Broadway stage must be covered with either paint or fabric, which is treated with fireproofing chemicals. The Scenic Designer must understand all of these materials and mediums.

The Scenic Designer must also understand shape, size and dimension. His imagination, drawings and renderings must translate into sets that fit into the stage space and that do not dwarf the actors or make it difficult for them to move around onstage or backstage. This is a big problem in most Broadway theaters because, historically, when many of the Broadway theaters were built, the shows were simple and required little wing or backstage space. Modern shows, however, are much more involved, with several large sets and many props that not only require space onstage, but backstage as well.

When space is limited, some scenery is temporarily hung in the air backstage by a system of chain motors and cable riggings until it is needed onstage. It is then lowered onto the deck and pushed out onto the stage for the scene—a sequence that is reversed and repeated throughout the show. A perfect example of this can be seen on the Disney show *The Lion King* which opened in 1997. There are approximately 25 quarter or half ton chain motors that lift most of the small scenery and prop and even wardrobe items off the deck. This is necessary for space, not only for other scenery, but also for the actors, the dressers and crew that need to move around freely backstage. Throughout the course of the show the activity backstage, with people moving about, as pieces of the scenery are lowered in, is a special type of choreography that the audience never sees. A Designer must take his space, the movement of his scenery and the movement of the cast and crew into account when deciding how much scenery to design and build.

If the show is small and the scenic requirements simple, then expenses and space and even upkeep are not a major problem. In 1984 Whoopi Goldberg burst upon the public scene with a one-woman show on Broadway. The scenery consisted of the bare stage, a few curtains and a couple of props. The show was simple to design, simple to construct, and easily maintained. With its small cast, simple set and basic crew it was also very inexpensive to run.

These shows are few and far between. These days, some Broadway shows have elaborate hydraulic sets and intricate and sometimes motorized props that end up being the most expensive elements of a production. Instead of simple and cheap it's almost like "bigger is better." For some Designers and producers, realism is important, as is spectacle. And realism and spectacle cost money.

After reading the script and talking to the writer, composer and director, the Scenic Designer determines the realm in which he will ply his trade. If the show is a historical piece, the Designer must be familiar with architectural and furniture styles of various periods. If no style or period guidelines are specified in the script, the Designer must rely on his imagination and research into known styles. All of the props that are handled by the performers—from teacups, umbrellas and suitcases to chairs, tables or pianos—are either designed and constructed or shopped for by the Scenic Designer or his staff. They too must fit into the style of the show. And, of course, the Designer makes all decisions on the colors and textures of his set, which puts to use his talents as a visual artist.

If the show happens to call for an outdoor set, then either real or fabricated trees, bushes, rocks or stone walls can be found or created. There may be a large scenery drop used as a background on which blue sky and clouds are painted, and mountains are visible in the distance. I remember creating a babbling brook on stage, complete with running water, for a Designer who wanted as much realism as possible for a play that took place in the woods.

The sets for all Broadway shows are built by Union carpenters and technicians (members of the International Alliance of Theatrical Stage Employees, I.A.T.S.E.) in Union sanctioned scenic shops. These technicians and carpenters follow the blue prints drawn by the Designer and/or his assistants and construct every piece of every set— with all the details. This construction is supervised by a lead carpenter or production carpenter and sometimes by the Designer himself. The Designer, incidentally, must be a member of the United Scenic Artists Union (USA 829) in order to design a show for Broadway.

Once all the construction is completed, a crew of scenic artists, who must also be USA members, paints and decorates the set according to renderings supplied by the Designer. Walls of steel and luan (thin plywood) can be painted to resemble a beautifully gilded wall from an 18th century home in Boston. The design team can then recreate a painting of the Mona Lisa to hang on the wall, flanked by two gas jet sconces that may actually work. In front of this wall may be an exact replica (either borrowed or built) of a sofa from the period, complete with footstool. Joined to this wall may be two other similar walls: the one on the right with French doors and the one on the left with a fireplace and mantelpiece. Top it all off with a suggestion of a ceiling complete with a chandelier and you have what is known as a "box set." Many shows are staged on this traditional type of set, which is in the shape of a box with one side missing, through which the audience views the show.

Once the show's scenery is built and moved into the theater, the Designer is on hand to solve problems. No matter how much thought and planning went into the design, there are many details left to be worked out in the theater when everything is put together. And as rehearsals ensue, the master carpenter, under the supervision of the Designer, coordinates the movement of the scenery during scene changes—onstage as well as offstage.

It is possible to re-create literally anything onstage. If it exists in the real world a good Designer can copy it and replicate it. If it doesn't exist in reality then the Designer's imagination creates it. The possibilities are endless. No matter how involved, expensive, simple or inventive the scenic elements are, it's the Scenic Designer's responsibility to create the best possible environment within which the actors and director can work their own theatrical magic. Like any other character in the show, the set and props can play an integral part in creating just the right atmosphere. Perhaps that is why, when the curtain first goes up, many times the scenery gets the first ovation.

After the show opens, the Scenic Designer may return occasionally to see that the set is holding up and functioning properly under nightly use. He may also supervise any major revisions of the set that are the result of wear and tear. Other than that, there is no official reason for him to be in the theater, so he will collect his weekly or monthly royalty check and move on to design a new show.

The Lighting Designer

The Lighting Designer is an artist too. His mediums are light and color, and his materials are specially designed lighting instruments and, of course, electricity. Just as the Scenic Designer must be an experienced carpenter, the Lighting Designer must be a qualified electrician.

It is the responsibility of the Lighting Designer to show off everything that must be seen during a performance, and, at the same time, hide everything that should be kept a secret. The LD can distinguish between night and day—and even dusk. On a bare stage he can make the audience feel as if they are either outside in the sun or inside a room with only one window. The LD can affect the mood of a performance by his use of light. He can create the sudden explosion of lightning or the soft glow of a candle. But, at all times, no matter what the mood or the setting, and no matter how many people are on stage, the LD must be sure that every performer is seen by the audience. After all, it is the relationship between audience and actor that is the essence of the theatre.

The Lighting Designer has at his disposal a wide range of lighting equipment and as the industry and its technology grows, so does the scope and application of this equipment. There are lighting instruments called fresnels, par cans and beam projectors that throw a wide flood of light for general illumination. There are instruments called lekos that throw a narrow shaft of light for very specific areas of focus. There are lighting instruments that flash on and off (strobes), and instruments that contain several colors of light to be mixed according to levels of brightness (x-rays or strip lights). There are even moving lights—instruments that can be programmed by computer to change direction and even color by remote control.

The different "colors" of light are achieved by the use of a film like plastic called gelatin or "gel" which can change ordinary white light into a virtual rainbow of colors by simply slipping a square of the gel into a slot in front of the light. The LD can even project onto walls and floors the images of trees, bushes, stars, clouds, windows, doors and even lightning bolts, by using a small metal cutout called a "gobo" that fits inside the lighting instrument near the internal lamp.

On Broadway today a Lighting Designer may use upwards of 800-1000+ lighting instruments on his design for one show. Each instrument has a specific purpose and the possibilities are limited only by the imagination of the Lighting Designer, the set, the space and the availability of electricity.

But what if there is no electricity? After all, theatre has been around longer that the light bulb. What did the

Lighting Designer use when Shakespeare first produced *Hamlet?* Well, in actuality, Shakespeare had no Lighting Designer. He didn't need one. The Globe Theater was an open-air theater with no roof and the audience either sat on blankets, cushions or benches or stood for the performance. Shakespeare performed his plays during the day with the sun as the only light source. The same held true, before Shakespeare, in ancient Greece, in the great open-air theater of Dionysus. You could say that the sun was the first lighting instrument and the greatest Lighting Designer of them all controlled its use.

As theatre progressed and moved indoors, the use of candles and lighted torches provided a rudimentary but adequate form of illumination. It wasn't until Thomas Edison's invention that theatrical lighting and Lighting Designers became more prominent in the business. Today the LD is essential to any legitimate theatrical production. Ironically, unlike any other artist in the theatre, the achievement of the Lighting Designer is at it's best when the light—the sources, the colors and the changes—go unnoticed, leaving only the mood or desired effect to be felt by the audience.

Similar to the procedure surrounding the Scenic Designer's work, when the lighting design for a show has been completed and approved, its specifications are sent to several lighting equipment companies for estimates and bids. The producer or general manager enters into a rental agreement with the company for the use of the equipment on a weekly basis.

All major lighting equipment rental shops are Union affiliated and just like carpenters who build the sets, all electricians who deal with putting the lighting equipment package together are members of I.A.T.S.E. – the Stagehands' Union. A Lighting Designer on a Broadway show must belong to the United Scenic Artists Union.

The Costume Designer

The Costume Designer is the third major team player who has a shared responsibility for the overall visual characteristics of the show. The Costume Designer is responsible for everything that each performer wears on his or her body: shirts and pants, skirts, tights, socks, jewelry, ties, hats, coats and even shoes. As was mentioned, many times the Scenic Designer will also design the costumes in an effort to achieve a unity of style, color and composition. This is not a general rule and only happens with certain Designers simply because of the workload involved.

In terms of job description, the Costume Designer's work follows that of the other Designers. She will read the script and have discussions with the director as well as the other Designers. She will develop a design theme and create renderings and even collect fabric samples so that others can visualize her ideas. She will either shop for or hand-make each costume—that is to say, her assistants will shop and a wardrobe construction house will make each costume. In modern shows dealing with current wardrobe styles many things can be purchased and fitted to the individual actor. In shows of an historical nature where accurate costumes must be constructed or in shows where costumes are unique, designs are executed from measurement to layout to fabric cutting and sewing to finished product.

For shows opening on Broadway, or Broadway shows going on tour, everything is created or purchased new for every actor in every show. Off-Broadway, Off-Off-Broadway, community, regional, stock and even college theatre Designers can take advantage of costume rental businesses that have warehouses filled with a wide variety of costumes from nearly every historical period. In many cases these warehouses maintain complete sets of costumes for very popular and often produced shows. Some of the available stock may even be the original costumes worn by various Broadway casts identified by original name tags. Many of the costumes that are rented have been altered thousands of times by hundreds of wardrobe staffs.

The capitalization for a Broadway show will include the construction and purchase of all of the wardrobe items. The running costs of the show will cover the daily laundry, dry cleaning and upkeep of the costumes as well as any new costumes that replace things that wear out or that are constructed for new members of the cast. Costuming a show can be very expensive and, considering authenticity and longevity, most Broadway shows spare no expense. In many instances, except for very elaborate costumes, there are duplicates to most wardrobe items so that they can be cleaned on a daily basis. This is particularly true for shirts and blouses and under garments (tights, dance belts, socks, slips etc.) which are washed daily. Outerwear pieces (pants, jackets, skirts) are sent to the cleaners every week. Understudies get their own set of costumes for the role(s) they might perform. There is very little sharing of wardrobe even if actors are the same size. This might happen when there is a special wardrobe piece that is unique and may have been expensive to acquire or make. No one ever shares undergarments or shoes.

In small theaters with little or no budgets, plays are usually produced that require few if any special costumes. Comfort and authenticity give way to what can be begged, borrowed or faked. Costumes seem to be the first thing to get minimized at budget meetings. Yet the constant maintenance of poor quality costumes can be even more expensive.

The first job I had, shortly after moving to New York, was that of a set and costume Designer for an Off-Off-Broadway show called *Pontiac*. It was the story of a great Native American who lived in the early 1700s. We had absolutely no budget. The set was easy. We painted a few platforms and benches that already existed in the theater, hung a few curtains and presto—scenery! Not much of a design, but very functional and inexpensive.

For the costumes we needed a bit more authenticity. Needless to say we cut a few corners. We borrowed loincloths from a college production of *That Scottish Play* which had been done in a primitive style, and with nothing else but make-up it was all the braves needed for the summer scenes. But, you guessed it; we had winter scenes as well. For this we used old shirts, ripping off the collars, and made leggings out of old slacks with the crotches cut out. Chunks of fabric were put together for blankets and outer wear. Strings of beads and other pieces of jewelry, borrowed from the performers, added some color and decoration. The robes and feathers and head dressing for Pontiac himself were literally scrapes of fabric found in boxes in the theater storeroom. I did make one sack dress for the one female in the show—also out of scraps of fabric. And, as I recall, the only money that was spent was for safety pins and thread. Surprisingly enough, it worked. And while this is not the kind of situation that a Costume Designer dreams of, it is often the experience of each Designer at the beginning of a career.

Back on Broadway the Costume Designer and her wardrobe supervisor oversee all aspects of the design and execution of the wardrobe. There are countless details. And the work isn't finished once a costume is purchased or constructed. There are fittings, and alterations and accessorizing and more fittings. When the production goes into dress rehearsals, the Designer and supervisor are in the theatre watching as everything is worn to see if there are any problems with mobility or wear and tear. And all costume changes are worked out with the dressers—down to the nearest second.

Again, as with the other Designers on Broadway, the Costume Designer must be a USA 829 member. All wardrobe supervisors who maintain the show, dressers who help change the costumes and seamstresses who mend the costumes are all members of the Broadway Wardrobe Union I.A.T.S.E. Local #764.

My experiences in wardrobe include being a dresser on the original *La Cage aux Folles* and the Wardrobe Supervisor for Harry Belafonte traveling on tour.

Other Designers

Though scenery, lighting and wardrobe are the three main design areas, and most shows can get by with three Designers or less, there may often be independent Designers responsible for other facets of special shows.

Many shows will have a Make-up Designer responsible for general as well as specialized make-up—like for the Phantom in *The Phantom of the Opera*. These Designers are knowledgeable artists in their own right regarding make-up and how to apply it for the best effect on the Broadway stage. It is easy to see why a Make-Up Designer was required on the Broadway show *Cats* or *The Lion King*. But even in a show like *42ND Street,* where there is no specialized make-up, the Designer helped each performer develop a make-up mask which was specific to their features and coloring. There are over 30 ensemble players in *42nd Street,* half of them women who, despite the fact that they use make-up in their daily lives, require assistance to style their make-up for Broadway. Once this make up is designed, the performer applies it every night of the show. Stars are very often afforded their own personal make-up person.

More than likely there is a Hair Designer responsible for wigs and hairstyles. Even though everyone has their own hair, the particular requirements of the show, in terms of both style and functionality, will need to be attended to. For example, in the period piece *Phantom of the Opera* there are some 100 different wigs for a cast of 36 performers. Several cast members, usually the chorus members who play several different parts, have several different wigs. This is done because in the fast pace of the show it is much quicker to put on a wig that has been styled ahead of time, that to re-style someone's own hair. Sometimes the Make-up Artist and Hair Stylist are one and the same or a member of the hair department functions as a make-up consultant.

One of the first real theatre jobs I had after moving to New York was a non-Equity tour of the musical *1776*. I played the delegate from Georgia, Dr. Lyman Hall. As is the case with this type of tour, the cast also functioned in other crew type jobs. Some of us helped to put the set up in each theatre, others prepped the costumes and others helped with luggage or hotel accommodations.   One of my unique responsibilities was attending to the hair/wig of the actor who played Benjamin Franklin. It was my job to dress his wig into his own hair so that it looked natural and characteristic of the familiar look we all know. It was a volunteer position. I didn't make any extra money. But I had fun doing it and it usually looked great and garnered many comments.

Many big musicals, like *My Fair Lady, La Cage Aux Folles, Ragtime* and *Sound of Music* even hire their very own Hat Designer. It may seem that this would be part of the job description of the Costume Designer, but on the big shows, where the hats are sometimes as elaborate as the costumes themselves, it is only efficient to hire a separate person. Broadway's premier hat Designer, Woody Shelp, was someone I considered a friend.

Last but not least is a Sound Designer who, at the very least, is responsible for equipping the show with the proper sound gear—speakers and microphones. In all Broadway musicals the performers all wear body mics to pick up and transmit their voices. A sound operator is hired to mix the show so that each microphone and each speaker is properly balanced allowing each member of the audience, no matter where they sit, to receive the same rich and complete sound experience. Very often the Sound Designer may incorporate sound effects and/or taped music into a show's sound design for special effects such as explosions, thunder, breaking glass or train whistles. Years ago these sound effects were found on record albums and cassette tapes and were played on machines at the particular moment that they were required on stage. This meant that an operator would actually turn on a tape machine at the proper time. Now all the particulars and peculiarities of the sound are handled by computer with preprogrammed sound environments and settings as well as electronic sound effects. And the sound operator is stationed at the rear of the audience behind a large mixing console where he monitors the show and adjusts the sound on a constant basis.

It all costs money: scenery, lighting, costumes, special effects, sound and props. If the show was capitalized intelligently, and the money exists for everything to be made correctly, then the technical elements can add immeasurably to the success of the show. If corners are cut and things are done cheaply, it is not only apparent to the eye, but repairs must be made on a routine and constant basis which could drain the budget and close a show prematurely.

Each Designer must know his own craft, inside and out, as well as have a more than passing knowledge in the other design areas in order to coordinate the elements. There must be communication between Designers as well as cooperation. They are the Design Team and their efforts, though individual and unique, must meld together into a cohesive whole.

I have designed a few sets in my time—back in college as well as Off-Off-Broadway. I designed costumes for a modern dance company for a while. I was responsible for the lighting for a touring company that played in high schools and colleges all across the country—this was "seat-of-the-pants" lighting because I had to contend with whatever the school provided and make it work for our show. I have never designed, nor do I expect to ever design, for Broadway but my limited design experiences has definitely enhanced my work as a Broadway stagehand.

Designers are a rare breed of artists in their own right. Their knowledge and their craft are greatly admired and sometimes envied. Tony Awards are presented for the efforts of exceptional Designers, and in fact, shows often win awards for design and nothing else.

Scene 6 : THE ACTOR

As stated before, a play exists only as a literary achievement until it is presented in front of an audience. True theatre happens when a living Actor personifies a writer's idea, guided by a director, in front of an audience who will, hopefully, be affected by what is seen and heard. The Actor is the instrument through which the written word is carried to the listening audience.

Without the Actor, the writer's words are just arrangements of letters—just a story to be read. Without the Actor the director has no one to direct. Without the Actor there is no one to wear costumes; no one to stand in the light; no one to walk on the set. Without the Actor . . . well, you get the message. The Actor is the one fundamental required element of the dramatic art form. Every other element depends upon the Actor for its existence.

Without the Actor there is no theatre.

Who is the Actor?

Anyone who possesses a need or desire to be expressive in front of an audience can try to be an Actor. This doesn't mean that anyone who attempts the acting profession will be successful, make a living, or even understand the first thing about what they are doing. But it does mean that anyone can try. And although thousands do try, year after year, audition after audition, very few actually make a career out of it.

Actors come from every walk of life. Some are born into the profession, following in the footsteps of show business parents. Some are "discovered" and have a career nearly thrust upon them. Some start their careers in school and progress from academic theatre to professional theatre as a studied career choice. Some enter the profession late in life perhaps after another career has run its course or failed. Some were once writers (or still are), never having been satisfied at how others performed their work. Many theatre producers and most directors have some acting credits somewhere on their resumes. Even some designers, stage managers, dressers and stagehands may have, at one time, taken a bow.

No matter where they come from, or what their motivations, there is one common denominator to their pursuit—an unexplainable desire. Some define this desire in terms of being accepted, or wanting to entertain. Some see fame or fortune. Some are drawn by an instinct that can't be verbalized. In fact, with all the pressure and traumas, broken promises and shattered dreams, and with far too few rewards and benefits, the pursuit of an acting career remains one of the most mystifying decisions ever made.

For most, the desire lies somewhere in the heart next to those other special loves—family, spouse and children—which also defy definition. It's like a first love that is never forgotten. It's special, magical and mysterious. It's unexplainable, unrealistic and unshakeable. It is a need—like life and breath itself! It's the greatest part of what is commonly referred to as the magic of theatre.

How does an Actor act?

There are as many different answers to this question as there are Actors. And most Actors couldn't explain it or don't even really know. There are hundreds of acting schools and even more acting teachers or coaches. Each has a set of theories, definitions, styles and methods. The process of acting is universal while at the same time very special and personal. It can come easy and it can be very difficult. An Actor may feel satisfied or at times even cursed. There can be success and there is surely failure. Where that special desire and need that we have mentioned leaves off, and success begins, depends on talent—and talent can be quite elusive and equally as difficult to define.

If acting talent comes naturally, it is called a gift. Yet it can be learned and developed like any other talent. If it is great, then it is called genius. Yet even if it is only good it is still honored and applauded. How an Actor acts is difficult to put into words, but when it happens it is as easily recognizable as the sun.

Books, and people who profess to be able to teach acting, all talk about certain methods and processes. If understood and followed, one can usually be "taught" how to act. It is similar to an art class or the study of a musical instrument where certain talents are taught. The real "how" is rooted in the gift of talent.

Acting is an art form. If you could ask Michelangelo "how" he painted the Sistine Chapel you might get two responses: 1) "I spent a lot of time on my back with lots of paint and lots of brushes," and 2) "I just did it." The question "How does an Actor act?" can be answered the same way. On the one hand there are physical gestures and facial expressions; there are vocal inflections and patterns of speech; there are mimicking skills and miming techniques; there is memory and movement. On the other hand there is observation, assimilation, perception, intuition and emotion. Some things can be learned, other things cannot. Some things have to do with craft; other things have to do with talent. And it is that very nebulous thing called talent that separates the good from the bad and is sought and cherished by anyone who calls himself an Actor. It is so special that it can elude most people who attempt an acting career, yet elevate others to a "super star" level of professional achievement. And there are hundreds of books on just this one subject alone!

The Acting Challenge

So, if we can't analyze *how* the Actor acts, can we describe *what* the Actor does—what his responsibilities are—while doing the acting thing? We can—in general terms. Because the process of acting is unique to each Actor, so the answer is not a neat and tidy one. Later we'll get into finding work and auditions and rehearsals etc.

Basically an Actor does three things: she interprets, she creates and she pretends. And to do these things well requires an awareness of human behavior as well as a certain fearlessness.

When given a role to play, the first thing the Actor must do is figure out who the character is and how that character relates to the world of the play. In most cases the Actor did not create the character, the writer did, and there were probably very specific reasons for doing so. It is the job of the Actor to interpret those reasons and intentions and bring the character to life.

The Actor looks for clues in the writing, and she asks many questions, such as: Why is this character in the play? How does she relate to the other characters? Does she like her husband, son or father? Is she happy? If not, why? Is she truthful or does she disguise her words and deeds in mystery? What is her occupation? What are her dreams? And the list goes on....

The answers to these and other questions help the Actor interpret what the writer is trying to say. And just as all of our words, actions and dreams make us who we are, each character is given similar characteristics by the writer. The Actor must learn them and then live them.

And she is limited by her talent, by the dialogue, by the locations of the play, by the scene structure and by other characters. She must fill out all the sketchy information that is given and, guided by the director, arrive at an image of what the writer had in mind.

Must the Actor's interpretation match the writer's? Not necessarily. Depending upon the leeway the writer gives, many times an Actor has freedom to mold and shape on her own. But there are always the limits of the scope of the play. It is not uncommon to find different interpretations of a single character by several different Actors. Shakespeare's *Hamlet*, for example, has been played by dozens of notable and not so notable Actors—both male and female. Each presentation was based on the Actor's interpretation of the writer's intent. And each was unique and valid. This leeway of interpretation is the result of the fact that Shakespeare, who may have intended that Hamlet be played in a very particular way, isn't around to explain his intentions.

Except for new shows on Broadway, it is rare to find the writer around with barrels full of explanations. This is the Actor's challenge. Based solely on sometimes sketchy information and her own unique array of talents, the Actor must "create" on her own. It can be the very reason that audiences come to see a particular Actor—to see her interpretation of a role. It is often the reason for revivals—to see how someone else does it. And it is why the theatre revolves around the Actor and what the Actor does.

Interpretation and creation go hand in hand. Given the writer's and the Actor's interpretations the Actor creates the image of a real living human being—a complete "person." Under the guidance of the director, she molds and shapes that person by personifying what the character possesses. Sometimes the created person is very similar to the Actor in personality. In this case the Actor simply expresses her own personality within the framework of the character. At other times the character and the Actor are as different as night and day, so the Actor must rely on her general knowledge of people to help her carry out her task.

She analyzes the physical, mental and emotional aspects of others, sifts through the knowledge and chooses the needed elements required to personify the desired character. The Actor literally takes on the physical, emotional and intellectual characteristics of another person.

At all times it is the Actor's intent to portray the given character in such a way that the audience understands not only what the character says and does, but also why she says and does it. In simple terms, she is a mimic—she pretends to "be" other people. She has each of us in her pocket and she pulls us out and puts us on when the need arises. She walks the way we do; talks the way we do; makes funny faces, laughs or gets angry at the same things we do; dreams our dreams and hopes our hopes;   battles our problems, meets our challenges and is frustrated with our shortcomings. And she does all of this on stage for us to see. That is why we, the audience, identify with her performance. That is why we laugh, cry and applaud—because we see ourselves mirrored in what she says and does.

The process of portraying a character on stage is not only daunting, it can be quite demanding as well. It is very physical in many respects. But what is really depleting, is the emotional and intellectual strain. Can you imagine having to recall painful thoughts about the loss of a loved one in order to express grief or depression in a character on stage—night after night—maybe for years! This is the Actor's challenge—her job. And yet, for all the stress and strain, doing the acting thing, though sometimes only momentary, gives to each Actor an undeniable satisfaction.

The Typical Struggling Actor

So far all of this talk about Actors has been theoretical and a bit idealistic. It is one thing to say that an Actor creates, like a painter or a sculptor. And all that interpretation, theory, need and desire stuff can get pretty heady. But what does it all really mean? What is it really like to lead an Actor's life? Of course, it goes without saying that, no two Actors lead identical lives. Every acting career is as unique as every Actor is. But we can talk about typical situations: about an Actor's day to day activities; the show-to-show routines; and the Actor-to-Actor (to non-Actor) relationships and get a pretty basic look at the life of a typical Actor.

It's obvious that there is a marked difference between the life of a "working" Actor and the life of a "non-working" Actor. Although each is pursuing the same goals, their day-to-day activities and their struggle can vary a great deal. We will explore the life of a "working" Actor later, but if one were to fabricate a hypothetical profile of a "typical" struggling Actor, it might read something like my own:

In 1974 I packed all my essentials into my powder blue VW bug and left my Midwest home and family just like hundreds of other aspiring thespians before me. I had a college degree and a great deal of educational theatre work in my pocket. (A typical Actor will do more shows in college that in an entire professional career.) I also just finished a summer Stock job in an outdoor theater in Chillicothe, Ohio doing the show *Tecumseh*. I was bitten by the strange acting "bug" (which causes an incurable fever), so armed with $2000 and a dream, I made a decision to seek my fame and fortune in the Big City—New York (along with the common parental disapproval).

Some people hook up with friends, who probably came from the same college the year before and crash on the floor for weeks and maybe months. I stopped off in New Jersey where several friends from *Tecumseh* went to school and I found a small apartment near the school. This gave me an opportunity to be close enough to New York, so I could get to the city and find an apartment and work, while I hung out with my friends, worked in the school pub and even acted in a show on campus.

In New York City I looked for what seemed an interminable length of time until I found a very small one-bedroom apartment in a fairly nice building on the Upper West Side. The rent was $800 per month and it would become my home.

Success, of course, does not come immediately. And so I began finding "survival jobs" lasting for varying lengths of time. I worked in a bakery, as a clerk with Saks Fifth Avenue and even drove a taxi cab. It is a constant struggle to make ends meet. I even considered a roommate but there just wasn't enough room.

Over the first year or two there were countless auditions and some call backs with as many rejections. Each audition was approached with hope and each rejection was easier to deal with than the last.

I landed a few roles in small Off-Off-Broadway shows, the tour with a non-Union production of *1776* and a season of four shows in an Omaha, Nebraska Dinner Theater (which got me the all important Actors' Equity Union card). Off-Off-Broadway only paid subway fare and while I was out of town I was forced to sublet my apartment (guaranteeing that my cat would be fed).

I moved into a new apartment by 1978 that was on a government Section 8 subsidy—so my rent was geared to my income and it made things easier. More auditions. More rejections. I started working in small theaters as a "techie" building scenery, hanging and focusing lights and being a stage manager. I even landed a job at the famed American Academy of Dramatic Arts as a staff stage manager.

Then, a week before my 30th birthday, I landed my first Broadway show. It was a small show and, unfortunately, it only ran for six weeks and what followed was another slump. A year went by without anything substantial and it seemed that my career was at a complete standstill. And the questions began. "Should I give up?" "Will it always be a struggle?" "Am I really any good?"

Fortunately (or unfortunately) I had tasted the life of a "working Actor" and I carried on. I had no choice. It's that old fever being persistent. It's the gambler's impulse—"maybe tomorrow," "maybe this one." And so it went.

There are no figures as to how many theatre people give up. There is no way to count them. I have personally known dozens of friends who have either changed careers completely or just "gone home." It happens to every type of theatre person in the business. There is no way to know if those who quit are happier now.

There are figures based on the 2007 Actors' Equity Association records that show that employment as an Actor is anything but inspiring. Out of approximately 47,000 national Equity members approximately 17,000 – 18,000 are working each year (38%).

6% earns more than $75,000/year in the theatre
4% earns between $50,000 and $75,000
11% earns between $25,000 and $50,000
10% earns between $15,000 and $25,000
29% earns between $5,000 and $15,000
and 40% earns less that $5000 (Poverty level being approx. $9,000/yr)

The median annual earnings per member is around $7,239.

Average weekly salary on Broadway is $2,229.

The average number of weeks worked per year is 17.

Yet, on the other side of this seemingly sad, desperate story, are theater marquees with Actor's names on them (some of them above the title). There are Tony Awards every season extolling the virtues of the theatre. There are occasional long running shows and TV and movie offers. There are people who begin to recognize you on the street. And there is the applause.

The life of an Actor (even a working Actor), or for

that matter, the life of any theatre person, is a deplorable struggle against seemingly insurmountable odds. The heartaches and frustrations are great; the rewards are few. But motivating it all is that burning desire, that special love, that incurable fever, that unexplainable need—to try.

Actors' Equity Association: Rules and Contracts

There are "Equity" Actors and stage managers and there are "non-Equity" Actors and stage managers. "Equity" Actors and stage managers are members of Actors' Equity Association (sometimes referred to as A.E.A. or simply Equity). Equity is the national labor organization that has jurisdiction over all Actors and stage managers that work in the professional theatre. All Actors and stage managers that are not members of Equity are called non-Equity (or non-Union). Actors who work in film are members of the Screen Actors Guild (S.A.G.). Actors who work in TV and radio are members of the American Federation of Television and Radio Artists (A.F.T.R.A.).

In general, there are only two major differences between Equity and non-Equity: Equity members are guaranteed certain minimum salaries, pensions and welfare, unemployment contributions, vacations and insurance coverage; non-Equity members are not. And Equity members can only work in Equity approved theaters where specific working conditions and rules are enforced; non-Equity people can work anywhere, however, they may only work in an Equity approved theater if they become a member of Actors' Equity or are in the Equity Apprentice Program.

There are certain advantages to both classifications, but most feel that the value of guaranteed minimum salaries and decent working conditions far outweighs any restrictions on the numbers of theaters one can work in.

Why is there a need for an Actors' Union? Because, like in other labor situations before Unions were organized, there were producers who made a habit of exploiting Actors and stage managers. Among other things, these producers would schedule long rehearsal hours, with no breaks. Rehearsals would be held in poorly heated and/or ventilated rooms with uncomfortable, if any, dressing rooms and often times, sub-standard restroom facilities. And there were little if any salaries! Profits would go right into the producers' pockets. Sometimes touring theatre companies would run out of money on the road and performers would be stranded in cities far from home with no money and no transportation. It sounds unbelievable but it's true.

So, in order for Actors to protect themselves from these and other unscrupulous practices, theatre professionals banned together in 1913 and refused to perform unless they got fair and professional working conditions—and their right to earn a living was guaranteed. Everyone who wished to be protected by those guarantees joined the Union. Needless to say, this made life difficult for a lot of producers of the bigger shows. It was felt, at that time, that Equity Actors and stage managers were the best Actors and stage managers. Though this statement is not always true, the converse does seem logical: those Actors that are seasoned and experienced and hence, more desirable, are *probably* Equity members. Producers soon realized that for a show to have a better chance of success, the best quality of Actor seemed necessary. Producers began to deal with Actors' Equity Association.

Today, in order to be permitted to employ Equity members, a producer or theater must be granted a charter by Equity, which sanctions that producer or theater as a legitimate bondable theatrical employer. Every Actor or stage manager that is employed at a theater or with a producer that is under Equity's jurisdiction must be signed to a bona fide Equity contract complete with all the guarantees.

Whether an Actor is chosen through auditions, is a personal friend of the musical director, or had the role specifically written for her by the writer, a contract must be signed before an Actor can begin rehearsals.

An Equity contract states, in basic terms, that the Equity member agrees to be prompt at all rehearsals; appear at the theater no later than ½ hour prior to each performance; and to perform her role or job to the best of her abilities. In return, the producer agrees to abide by all the rules and regulations set down by Equity and to pay the performer the appropriate salary for the "use" of her talents or services.

There are two types of standard Equity contracts guaranteeing minimum salaries: the Principal contract—for anyone who speaks dialogue in a musical or a straight play; and a Chorus contract—for performers who only sing and dance in a musical. All stage managers and assistant stage managers sign Principal contracts.

Basically there are only two situations where salaries above the minimum are paid: when a performer negotiates with the producer for more money (i.e. a star or a featured dancer); or when an ensemble member or chorus member is assigned extra dialogue, is asked to do risky physical business, or understudies a role.

At the time each contract is signed, any and all riders to the contract must be signed as well. Any special agreement or arrangement, between the producer and the performer, that is not in conflict with any Equity rule—but may not be covered by the standard rules—must be put into a rider attached to the contract. For example, if an Actor is requested to cut her hair extremely short, or dye it another color, and maintain it that way for the duration of her employment, then that agreement must be in writing. Star billing, special dressing rooms and limousines all can be guaranteed by a rider in the contract. No agreement can exist unless it is in writing. The rule of thumb is if it isn't in writing—it isn't!

A performer who is not a member of Equity can become a member of Equity simply by being offered an

Equity contract. Then it is a simple matter of paying an initiation fee, and yearly membership dues and the Union membership and conditions are guaranteed.

Actors' Equity has jurisdiction over all shows on Broadway, Off-Broadway and on National and Bus & Truck tours. Equity also has jurisdiction over most Dinner Theaters, Summer Stock Theaters, Regional Theaters, Children's Theatre, Industrial Shows and, to a limited degree, Off-Off-Broadway. There are some non-Equity Dinner Theaters, Summer Stock and Regional Theaters that only employ non-Equity people. Some Industrials hire performers from other Unions and Equity membership is not required to do an Off-Off-Broadway show (in fact this is where struggling Actors usually get their start).

Some of the contract rules and guarantees that have been developed over the years (similarly in other Unions) include such things as: minimum salaries, length of rehearsal period, lunch and rest breaks, costume cleaning, dressing room and rest room requirements, conditions of dance floors, overtime pay, number of performances per week, publicity, photographs, sick leave and workman's compensation—to name a few. There is even a rule that specifies 30 inches of dressing table space for each performer. Hospitalization and medical insurance for members and their dependents, contributions to a pension fund and unemployment insurance are all paid for by the employer and guaranteed by the Equity contract.

Not all the current rules were instituted back in 1913. Every few years Union contracts with producers and theaters are re-negotiated. As society and the nature of the theatre business changes, so do the extent and particulars of the Equity contract. With each negotiation there may be major rule changes or only slight alterations to existing rules. Salaries are upgraded along with the cost of living. All rule changes are automatic and apply to all currently running shows.

If rules and contracts did not exist, there would still be the unscrupulous producer who would disregard the integrity of the Actor in order to fill their own bank accounts. I've witnessed first hand the extent that producers will go. The list of arbitrations decided against producers fill shelves in the Equity archives. That is why the Unions were formed—to protect the labor force.

I got my Equity card as a Dinner Theatre stage manager back in 1977 in Omaha, Nebraska. I subsequently stage managed in a variety of venues including Broadway. And I also acted—though my acting career didn't ever pan out. I stopped pursuing an acting/stage managing career after I was accepted into the stagehand Union's apprenticeship program and became a stagehand—but I maintained my membership in Actors' Equity until my retirement.

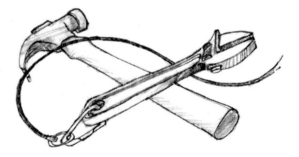

Scene 7 : THE CREW

The creative team and the production staff, as well as the performers, are all talented people whose work directly affects not only the look of the show but also the successful outcome of the show. Either directly or indirectly, the work of these people is on view nightly as each new audience comes to the theater. But no show would ever be mounted or maintained on an 8 show per week schedule without its behind-the-scenes backstage Crew.

Who are they?

The backstage Crew is an eclectic mix of people. Some of these professionals work in the theatre because they are pursuing a career in another area of the business and this is a way to keep from starving. Some are in the business because their fathers or uncles or cousins before them gave them work. And some do it simply because they love the theatre. Some Crew members love what they do. Others just need the money. They are men and women ranging in age from 18 to 65+, many of them married with children, some with college degrees; some with barely more than a high school diploma. They are of all races and creeds and philosophies, and they all work together to help make each and every performance run as smoothly as possible.

Most of the professional people who are part of the backstage Crew perform their jobs with very little credit, but, except for the actors themselves, nothing that is seen onstage gets there without the direct involvement of a member of the backstage Crew. They push and pull, they lift and carry, they assemble and dismantle, they work on their knees, they work up on platforms, they climb up and down stairs or ladders and walk back and forth across the stage to be in the right place at the right time so that each piece of scenery, each lighting instrument, each costume or prop gets to where it needs to be at the right time, so the show runs without faltering. They do the hard work so that others can take the glory. And they do it quietly and in the dark.

It is not unusual that the number of Crew people on a show outnumber the cast size by a ratio of two to one. On big Broadway musicals it is common for the size of the Crew to reach 40 or 50 people. They all have their individual specific jobs within their particular field and they do the same duties night after night from before the show until after everyone else goes home.

The members of the backstage Crew fall into job descriptions related to the design areas that we have discussed. There are carpenters and prop people who work with the scenic elements. There are electricians who work with the lighting and the sound. And there are wardrobe people who deal with the costumes, as well as hair and make-up people. Once the show is up and running, and the designers and their design teams have moved on to the next show, it is the backstage Crew that is left to operate and maintain all of the scenic and technical elements of the show.

Carpenters build, maintain, assemble and move all the large scenic elements such as platforms, step units, walls, backdrops, curtains, turntables and trap doors. These scenic elements are strictly part of the scenery and are not handled by the performers.

Prop people handle and maintain all the small scenic elements that actors actually *use* onstage, such as tables and chairs, books, lamps, pillows, plates, silverware, umbrellas, newspapers and puppets & bird kites (as in *The Lion King*).

Electricians maintain, move and operate the lighting equipment—either by operating a lighting console that controls the lights, by operating a follow spot, or by moving various lighting instruments around on the stage for use in specific scenes. Electricians are also responsible for maintaining and running the sound department. They monitor the speakers, hand out the individual body mics (small unobtrusive microphones) used by the performers, and operate the sound console that controls the speakers and microphones.

The wardrobe staff maintains all of the costumes including repairing, laundering and dry cleaning. They also function as dressers who assist the performers when they must change costumes either in their dressing rooms or quickly backstage between scenes. Hair and make-up . . . does hair and make-up.

Special effects can fall into either the carpentry or electric departments depending on the nature of the special effect—whether it is electrified or not. Sometimes a prop person will handle a special effect like the magic noose in *Phantom of the Opera.*

On each Broadway show there is a Production Crew (or Show Crew) as well as a House Crew. The Production Crew consists of department heads in the carpentry, electric, prop and wardrobe departments who are hired by the show's producer to maintain the show. The House Crew consists of a head carpenter, head electrician, and head prop person who are hired by the theater owner and who are responsible for maintaining the theater itself and for hiring the general Crew members who work on the show in the various departments. There is no House wardrobe head. The Show's wardrobe supervisor, hired by the producer, hires the wardrobe Crew.

All Broadway carpenters, electricians, sound and prop people are members of the International Alliance of Theatrical Stage Employees (I.A.T.S.E.). The members of the House Crew are all members of New York Local #1 of I.A.T.S.E. while the Production Crew can be members of any of the other National Locals (including even Local #1).

Broadway wardrobe personnel are all members of the I. A. Wardrobe Union – New York Local #764. These Unions have signed collective bargaining agreements with The League of American Theatres and Producers which is the general negotiating group that represents all Broadway producers and general managers. All Union salaries, health insurance, pension, annuity and working conditions are negotiated every few years. Payday is every Wednesday for the House Crew and every Thursday for the Production Crew and Wardrobe department.

Shops

As I have mentioned before, all of the visual and technical elements of each Broadway show are engineered, constructed, assembled, painted, and in the case of the wardrobe, cut, fitted and sewn, in one of the many Union shops that specialize in work specific to Broadway shows. In fact, no Broadway show can use scenery or lighting equipment that has not come from a Union shop. And the Crews in Union shops are all members of the various aforementioned protective Unions.

The scenic shops are responsible for using the designs of the scenic designer, which have been translated into blueprint drawings, to build and engineer all of the scenic elements. This may be as simple as constructing a wall with a window in it, or as complex as the telescoping three dimensional "Pride Rock" that rises out of the basement every night during *The Lion King*. During pre-production, the scenic designer has measured and taken inventory of the particular theater and its elements and has scaled his designs to fit. Prior to moving to the theater, all of the scenery is constructed and actually assembled in the shop so that every detail can be inspected and checked. Then it is dismantled and trucked to the theater. The carpenters and technicians in these shops are masters in their fields. They have built beautiful Broadway sets and engineered the most amazing scenic elements that have been thrilling audiences for 100 years on Broadway.

Electric shops are charged with putting together all of the lighting instruments and equipment that is rented by the Broadway shows. This includes the hundreds of specially designed theatrical lighting instruments, the miles of electrical cable, the multitude of plugs and jumpers and two-fers and gel frames or scrollers and gel and gobos and c-clamps and safety cable and hanging pipe and couplings and dimmer racks and control boards. All of it is put into specially designed crates or road boxes, which are trucked (by Union drivers) to the theaters. Unlike scenery that is created specific for a particular show, and is usually discarded when the show closes, the lighting equipment is rented on a per week basis and returned to the shops to be used on subsequent shows. All of the people who work in lighting shops are Union members.

Sound shops put together the equipment designated by the sound designer and this equipment is also rented on a weekly basis. Speakers, microphones, cable, etc. all get packaged, by Union employees, to be trucked to the theaters and returned when the show closes.

And all of the wardrobe is either purchased from stores (if modern dress is appropriate) or cut, fitted and sewn in costume shops by seamstresses who take the designs of the costume designer and magically change them into the unique and beautiful wardrobe that is seen on the Broadway stage.

All of this shop work is often begun before the show actually moves into the theater. And, except for wardrobe, even before the cast has been assembled or the rehearsals have started. Sometimes a Broadway show can take months to build in the shops. Workers labor from 8am till evening depending on the amount of work to do. The production carpenter, electrician and prop person make daily visits to the shops to monitor and oversee the progress of the work, to answer questions and solve problems as they arise.

Load-in

Just as the phrase suggests, the load-in is the time when the physical elements of the show move into the theater. As you can imagine, this doesn't happen in a day or two. And while it may happen in a week or two, it usually takes about a month depending on the size of the show. As has been mentioned, the producer of the show has rented the theater on a weekly basis for as long as the show will run. It is called a "four wall" rental and that is all that the producer expects to see on the first day. When the doors are open on the first morning of the load-in, the theater stage is bare.

Spotting lines is the first and only thing that happens during the first several days of a load-in. The carpentry Crew under the supervision of the show's master carpenter handles this. Every piece of scenery, lighting or sound equipment that hangs above the stage: curtains, walls, backdrops, scrims, lights, speakers—all must hang from long steel pipes that run the width of the stage or pipe ladders that hang vertically in the wings. The locations of the pipes are carefully laid out on the stage floor. The pick up points for each pipe are "spotted" and marked with tape or chalk on the stage deck. Enough space is allowed between pipes to accommodate what is being hung on them. These pipes are then, one by one, suspended by steel cables that run from the pipes up through steel pulleys (called sheaves) that are secured in place on the theater grid, and across to the fly floor and the arbor or hemp counterweight system. The process is slow and tedious and the carpenters must know what they are doing in terms of weight and cable strength, or they risk a serious problem if something breaks loose and falls.

Next the scenery and lighting equipment arrives at the theater and for the next several days or more there is a whirlwind of controlled confusion and activity. There are carpenters trying to hang the scenery and electricians trying to hang the lighting equipment and the sound Crew trying to hang the speakers. Sometimes they all want to be in the same place at the same time. There are dozens of Crew members with various tools on their belts and they are all over the theater. They are working from electric genie lifts high over the deck and they are working from ladders out in the house over the seats.

Sometimes it appears to be so chaotic that there are doubts that anyone knows what to do, or at least what to do first. There are pieces of the set lying about, a wall structure here and a platform unit over there. There are curtains and stacks of wood and lighting instruments in every aisle, in every row of seats and every corner of the theater. There are tools and saw horses and ladders invariably in someone's way. There is electric cable running from one lighting instrument to another, some of it dangling from ceiling to floor, looking like a mess of twisted black spaghetti. There are saws and hammers and drill guns being used—not only to put the set together, but also to "fix" it when it doesn't fit together like it was designed to fit. And the electricians hanging the lights have their crescent wrenches tied to their belts so that while working high up on ladders, the wrenches won't fall and fracture a skull. Though it seems like chaos, there is an order to it all. Certain things need to be done in a certain order and the department heads, who are constantly monitoring the progress of events, work all this out.

The prop Crew is busy setting up the areas in the theater basement where the various departments will cluster their equipment. They are moving metal cabinets and lockers around. They are making shelves for props and other equipment. They are setting up dressing rooms with chairs and Equity required cots. They may be setting up the orchestra equipment if the show is a musical and they are keeping the trash in the theater from piling up on the floors or in the trash cans. The actual props and wardrobe generally don't arrive in the theater till the second or third week of the load-in. The props are generally set aside out in the house to keep them safely out of the way while the major construction is still going on. The wardrobe goes to the basement in an area set aside for the wardrobe department. Sometimes the wardrobe department may be located in one of the larger dressing rooms.

After nearly everything is hung in the air over the stage, the show deck can be laid in. Shows generally do not perform directly on the stage floor because invariable there is scenery that needs to track on and off the stage by winches and cables. The 12 inch show deck is built to accommodate the tracks and cable pulleys, and there may be a turntable and several trap doors. Piece by piece this deck must be laid down carefully so that all of the tracks and hardware line up and so that the deck is all level and solid when walked on. Obviously no one can be working on this deck while it is being put together. That is why the equipment in the air is hung first.

Every day of the load-in starts with clearing areas of the stage that need to be worked on. All of the equipment boxes are usually pushed out onto the street and lined up outside the theater. The show department heads discuss the day's activities and the house heads assign the Crew tasks. It seems like there is always chaos and that someone is always in someone's way. And it also seems that everyone claims proprietary rights to time and space. But this is just the nature of the load-in. There is a lot to be done. There are dozens of people working all over the theater. Safety concerns are rigidly adhered to. Coffee breaks happen at 10am and at 3 pm and, for the first week or so, the workday may end at 5 pm. When the schedule gets closer to the arrival of the cast for the beginning of stage rehearsals, then the load-in Crew may work until 10 pm in the evenings. The last thing that happens every night is the bringing in of all the equipment that has been sitting out on the street.

The stage is taking shape. The scenery is all in and assembled. The scenic artist (who works for the scenic designer) may appear to touch up the scenery that got scuffed in transport. The lighting equipment is all hung and the lighting designer arrives to conduct focus calls where each individual lighting instrument is pointed in the direction for which it was designed. Props are unpacked and stored on shelves or hung on cable motors above the stage in the wings. The wardrobe Crew is busy organizing and dispersing all of the costumes to the various dressing rooms. The sound Crew checks out the microphones and speakers to make sure they all work.

Gradually the load-in morphs into tech rehearsals. The Crew is generally cut down from the large number needed to put the show into the theater to a smaller number necessary to run the show. There is still a lot of work to be done on the sets and lights, and this usually happens in the mornings. The cast is now coming to the theater for rehearsals, which usually take place in the afternoons and evenings. Slowly but surely everything is coming together and heading for opening night.

Running Crews

By the time the audience starts coming to Previews, the Crew consists only of those who will have a regular job on the show for as long as the show lasts—the running Crew. The size of the running Crew varies from show to show and from department to department. A show with a great deal of scenery will have extra carpenters. There are between two and six fly men who handle the ropes and lower and raise the flying scenery drops or other equipment. One or two technicians on the automation Crew are responsible for the computers that operate all of the automated scenery that either flies in or tracks onto the stage by winches and cables. And there are several carpenters on the deck to move rolling scenery around.

There will be electricians on the deck as well, moving certain lighting instruments or light towers that need to be in different locations at different times during the show. If the show is a musical, there are follow-spot operators. There is a light board operator and, these days, with the use of more and more programmable moving lights, there is an electrician specifically hired to operate and fix them. There are three of four sound men dealing with the microphones and running the sound board.

Members of the prop Crew are stationed on either side of the stage to handle the props. They keep all of the props organized and within easy reach for the actors to pick up from various shelves strategically located in every nook and cranny. The prop Crew is also very busy moving larger prop items around, as well as on and off the stage.

Sometimes there are two dozen or more dressers on big shows. Each star has a personal dresser and there is a whole crew of dressers responsible for all of the costume changes for the rest of the cast. They carry costumes on hangers and baskets of costume pieces all around the stage and in the basement and up in dressing rooms and in stair wells—wherever it is convenient for a quick costume change to take place. At times there are as many dressers backstage as there are all other Crew members. On *42nd Street* there were over 30 dressers.

The stage Crew is required to be in the theater by "half hour" before each show. They set up the scenery and props for the beginning of the show and the wardrobe Crew get the costumes ready. Usually the wardrobe Crew, and very often the running Crew, will be required to arrive an hour earlier. This happens because on some shows a half an hour of time before the curtain goes up isn't enough for the Crew to get everything checked and ready.

Stage Crew members can leave after they do their last cue—even before the end of the show. Wardrobe stays till the end because they must deal with the costumes after the show.

Everything that a Crew member does during the course of a show is called a "cue." All of the cues are worked out during tech rehearsals and assigned to each Crew member as the need arises. Sometimes a major cue like the moving of large scenery is signaled to happen by the stage manager who turns off a cue light. But most of the time the Crew members just remember when things happen, usually connecting it to dialogue or music onstage, and repeat the moves in sequence every night. In total, a Crew member's set of cues is called his or her "show" or "track." When a Crew member is out sick or on vacation a substitute Crew member is hired to fill in and do that particular show or track—because the work that needs to be done requires the same number of Crew people for every performance.

There are additional people who don't work backstage, but who are equally necessary to the smooth operation of the show on a nightly basis. Some are called the front-of-house Crew. They are the house manager and various assistants, the box office staff, ushers and concession people, and the housekeeping Crew. These people are hired by the theater owner and usually work in their positions on every show that is running in their theater. Aside from the house manager and assistants and the box office staff, these are usually minimum wage positions. I.A.T.S.E. Local #306 covers this jurisdiction with appropriate rules and regulations.

There are also doormen, and theater engineers, hired by the theater owner, who are in the theater every day and every night maintaining the operation and security of the theater itself.

Work Calls and Rehearsals

Things wear out. Things break. When this happens, things need to be fixed. Most of the time fixing things can't happen during a show. So a special work call is scheduled to do any work that needs to be done—fixing things that are broken and even preventative maintenance so things don't break as often. This work call is often scheduled on a regular basis on Wednesday mornings before the Wednesday matinee. Or a Thursday or Friday can be set aside for major work that needs to be done—which can't be accomplished in the 4 hours on Wednesday mornings.

The running Crew is called in for these work calls. It's extra money so everyone is grateful for it. Sometimes extra outside people come in for special work. Scenic artists may come in to repaint portions of the scenery. If a major scenic piece is being replaced, extra crew members may be called in or members from the shop that built the piece may come in to assist.

Big shows require a lot of maintenance to keep them running. The last thing anyone wants to have happen is a piece of scenery or a prop failing to make it onstage at the appropriate time. And no one wants to have to stop the show to fix something that breaks. While these surprises sometimes occur, preventative work calls can usually keep things on track.

The wardrobe department has a work call every day. It's called "day work." This is the time when the laundry and ironing happens and the general upkeep of the costumes. Not every dresser has day work but most want it because it means, once again, extra money.

During the run of a show, there are always rehearsals. Usually each week on Thursday and/or Friday understudy rehearsals are held to give the understudies an opportunity to keep up on roles that they may need to perform. They need to be ready to "go on" at a moment's notice. And when cast members leave the show, they are replaced with new actors who need replacement rehearsals to learn their roles.

When a cast member is scheduled to "go on" for a leading role, he or she may get a "put in" rehearsal. Crews attend these rehearsals on a need basis. Usually with ordinary understudy rehearsals, there are two prop people to deal with the show props because these things cannot be used without a Crew member present. On larger "put in" rehearsals the entire running Crew, including wardrobe people, is called in.

Load-out

You guessed it. During the load-out, everything that was brought into the theater, way back at the beginning, has to be taken *out* of the theater. The load-out might happen only a few short months after it all began—for limited run shows or for shows that close soon after opening. Or it might not happen for many years, as in the case of the closing of *Cats* in September of 2000 after an 18 year run.

What happens in the load-out is basically the reverse of what happened during the load-in—only a little faster. Everything comes down a lot quicker that it went up. A load-out usually only takes a week or two to accomplish. While safety is always an issue, dismantling scenery doesn't have to be a careful process. Unless the scenery is being saved for possible use elsewhere—like on a tour, the Crew simply cuts it up into pieces to be carted away in trucks. Props and pieces of furniture that are usable are stored for later use. Some items may be sold or given away to cast members as souvenirs. Wardrobe is shipped to wardrobe storage houses.

When the load-out is complete, the theater will once again look as it did the first day the show began its load-in— empty but for the bare walls and stage floor—ready for the next show and the next Crew to begin the process all over again.

Scene 8 : THE SHOW

N ow let's put the Show together. This is the routine. This is the "work" that theatre people do. We say that an actor "has a Show" and her "job" will be to learn the songs, dance routines and dialogue while "in rehearsal." And she will go to the theater and "do the Show" every night for as long as the Show "runs."

This is theatre; this is the process that every Show that is ever produced goes through. There are, of course, many individual differences from Show to Show, from cast to cast and from theater to theater. But in general, whether it is Broadway or Dinner Theatre, a play or a musical—every Show gets produced, rehearsed and performed in much the same fashion.

We've discussed the various elements—the people and their jobs—now we will take a typical hypothetical Show and see how all of these elements, and more, fit together.

Pre-production

You will recall that it all starts when the producer discovered and "bought" the writer's book and the composer's score. He formed a limited partnership and raised the necessary capital required to "go into production." Then the producer hired his production staff (if he didn't already have them), and the Show's artistic staff, and everyone set about their jobs and responsibilities. Prior to any actor signing a contract, even before auditions, the wheels and gears of the production were already in motion.

This period of activity, before rehearsals get underway, is called *pre-production.*

Although the script and score are essentially finished, the writer and composer may be discussing some rewrites with the director. The composer (maybe also the lyricist) is probably working on the orchestrations with the assistance of a musical director. Harmonies and vocal parts are being roughed in until casting takes place and real voice capabilities can be considered.

The choreographer is listening to the music over and over again. This, along with discussions with the director, is feeding the choreographer's imagination such that fragments of routines and dance steps are beginning to take shape.

The designers are busy researching, discussing, sketching, discussing, choosing equipment and fabric, discussing—on and on, until creativity blooms and the individual designs begin to evolve.

Negotiations have been underway with a star or two and contracts are being drawn up outlining salary, billing, length of contract and perks. If the publicity agent is cunning, there may already be a story or two leaked to the press about "so and so starring in such and such."

Arrangements for the rental of the theater have already taken place and are being finalized. This happens early, even while another Show may be running in the designated theater, because the designers are severely limited if they don't know what the theater looks like. Since each Show is hopeful of a long run, Broadway theaters draw up rental agreements that are open-ended. The producers for our Show wanted a specific theater and, as it happens, there was already a Show in the theater which was closing soon because of slowing ticket sales. The designers are able to see the theater and make measurements that will aid them in their work.

Even though our producer has cleared capitalization, additional investors are being pursued to sweeten the bankroll and safeguard against unforeseen expenses. Supplies are being purchased, a rehearsal hall rented, crews being formed, props being gathered, scripts and music copied, rehearsal schedules outlined. All of this and more happens even as auditions are just getting under way. Once the cast is chosen, then it is full steam ahead into production.

Into Production

Up until now it's all been about preparation and getting ready—setting up the business and hiring the personnel. Once the cast is chosen, our Show goes "into production." For the next several weeks all the focus is on putting all the elements of the Show together in rehearsals with the cast, and in the shops with the technical elements. When it is time to move into the theater, all of the elements and crews will come together in the same place and work like dogs to get our Show ready for opening night!

Generally, rehearsals don't begin until the full cast is hired and signed to contracts. But sometimes rehearsals begin with one or two cast members still to be determined. Since everything is on a tight schedule, with studios and theaters rented and opening night set, rehearsals begin with any last minute cast additions filling in as soon as possible.

A rehearsal period can last anywhere from ten days to several weeks or months depending on how big and complicated the Show. Many Dinner Theaters and Summer Stock Theaters rehearse for as few as ten days. But these theaters generally produce well-known Shows and in many cases hire casts who have performed in the Shows before.

A new Show, especially a Broadway musical, needs much more time. Six to eight weeks is an average rehearsal period. Big musicals will rehearse longer, smaller non-musicals will rehearse less. A producer who doesn't schedule or can't afford adequate rehearsal time, may be opening his

Show before it is ready, and may be cutting his own throat.

The first three weeks of rehearsal for our Show are scheduled to take place at "890 Studios"—named for its address on Broadway at 19th Street. Many Broadway Shows begin rehearsals here, ever since the late 70s when *A Chorus Line* director Michael Bennett opened the studios. There are several other rehearsal studios in New York City like the Minskoff Studios and the New 42nd Street Studios and the studio rental business does quite well. Studios charge on a per-day or per-week rental basis, depending upon the studio size and location. Sometimes it is as hard to book a rehearsal studio as it is to book a theater.

Studios are large open rooms from 500 square feet to as large as 4000 square feet usually containing a wall of mirrors, a piano and sometimes a dance barre. The floor of a studio that rents to Broadway Shows must be "dancer safe" (according to Equity rules) which means it must "give" to cushion a dancer's jumps and leaps. Our hypothetical Show has rented 3 studios at "890" where the book, dance and music rehearsals can take place simultaneously.

According to Equity rules, the length of a rehearsal day cannot exceed 8 ½ hours, out of which an hour and a half is for lunch—although the cast can elect to take a one-hour lunch. Lunch must come after no more that five hours of rehearsal and there must be a five minute break, every hour, all day long. Equity also requires that the cast have one day off after every six days of work. There are special 10-hour rules for the length of rehearsal days just prior to the first public performance; for rehearsals during previews (performances in front of audiences prior to opening night); and rehearsals called after opening for understudies and replacements.

And, in addition to the time actors actually spend in the rehearsal studio, there is always the homework—learning the dialogue and the lyrics and the choreography. This homework is not specifically assigned as in school, but it is understood that a professional actor will be prepared for every rehearsal. Eight, ten, as much as fourteen hours of rehearsal and homework on some days is not a rarity. The rehearsal period is perhaps the busiest, most challenging and certainly the most tiring time for an actor. Theatre is definitely a full time occupation!

Rehearsals: The First Day

The stage managers arrive at the studios several days before the first day of rehearsals. They will set up what can be considered a fully functioning office, complete with phone, computer, filing boxes, and all the office supplies necessary. They will also set up the studio with folding tables and chairs and tape the outline of the set on the floor with different colored tape marking different scenes. The production prop person has collected some of the props and furniture for the Show or has had facsimiles made at the scenic shop, and has transported them to the studio, so that rehearsals can be conducted with many of the props that will be used in the Show.

The first day of rehearsal is both calm and chaotic. The general atmosphere is very relaxed and extremely friendly. Even though the director, the stage manager and the producer are the only people who know everyone present, several members of the cast will recognize each other from auditions and callbacks or other Shows. But, for the most part, the cast and the staff are meeting each other for the very first time. Since everyone has signed a contract, there is no more competition. Everyone has a job and is looking forward to the work. There is a common bond. In a unique way, everyone is both stranger and friend.

When everyone has arrived it's down to business.

The stage manager hands out what seems to be an endless supply of material and information: scripts, rehearsal and production schedules, cast and crew contact sheet, insurance cards, pension and welfare cards, W-4 forms, publicity information, ticket policy information, costume measurement forms, program biography forms and more. Most of the material is self-explanatory; some is explained by an Equity representative who may be invited to answer questions for the first few minutes of the first day.

After "Equity business" is taken care of, the producer will say a few words of welcome and perhaps introduce the designers and other staff members who are present. The director will talk a little bit about the Show and his concepts for this production. Ditto the musical director and choreographer. Then, often with new Shows, the cast will gather around a large table or circle of chairs and begin to read and/or talk through the script for the first time as a cast. As the read-through progresses, the director will interject comments about characterization, motivation and perhaps scenery and costumes. Chances are that the set designer has built a scale model of the set, or at least has some drawings or renderings that the director can refer to as the reading proceeds.

This first read-through could be a very comical situation, especially since, on new Shows, it is probably the first time the cast has seen the script. The funny lines are funny for the first time. The music is charming for the first time. The climax is suspenseful for the first time. A composer, singing his own songs, can be quite entertaining. The producer, director and writers are paying close attention. As the actors are speaking, laughing and listening, they are beginning to create characters. The spontaneity, though entertaining, may also point out flaws and areas that need work. Because, beginning now, the creative team will tear the script apart scene by scene, line by line, note by note, analyzing and searching for the best possible Show. The funny lines may lose some humor, the music will become repetitious and the climax will lose its suspense—all in an effort to make the Show spontaneous again.

As this first work-through continues, other activities are taking place. The costume designer, or an assistant, may be collecting some measurements from various cast members. Perhaps the press agent is floating around trying to arrange press dates with a star or the director or the writer. The stage manager is beginning to take notes on such things as props and scene changes and possible costume and light changes. If the producer has stayed for the read through, he is probably dealing with business as he listens. Assistants are scurrying around with phone messages, memos, lists and bills to approve and soon it's time for lunch.

After lunch the stage manager will conduct the "deputy" elections. Since the Equity representative cannot be on the scene every day, an Equity deputy is elected by the company of actors to make sure that no contract rule is violated, and to represent the group in any dispute between labor and management. There is a small stipend granted to the elected deputy, and the position holds considerable weight in the eyes of the Union. If a problem can't be solved first by the stage manager, or by the deputy, then the deputy takes the matter to the Union.

After the election, rehearsal resumes. If the read through was not completed before lunch, then it continues. As soon as it is finished work begins. The director will begin preliminary blocking rehearsals in one studio and the choreographer will begin dancing with the chorus in another. The musical director works with individuals and groups of singers as the schedule permits—grabbing people as he can. It is the job of the stage manager to shuffle all the needs and to schedule rehearsals in such a way that everyone's time is used efficiently and no one is either sitting around or over worked. It is not an easy task.

When the work begins, all of the extra people disappear. Producers, designers, assistants bid the cast adieu and take their leave. During work, it is not customary to have extra people hanging around.

At the end of the first day of rehearsal there is an unexplainable, uncontrollable sense of excitement in the air. People don't rush out the door when work is over. They linger. Two or three may even continue working. Friendships are beginning to form. It is a business where the workers can't seem to get enough of the work. This eagerness and devotion is part of the magic of theatre. If the doors of the studio must be closed, the stage manager may literally have to throw some lingering cast members out.

Rehearsals: The Grind

For those performers with Principal (leading) roles, the first week or so of rehearsals is very busy. There is dialogue to memorize; scenes must be blocked; and music, lyrics and dances must be learned. On any given day, an actor will be rehearsing portions of her role with the director, the musical director and the choreographer—and on some days—all three.

The first week or so of rehearsals is always slow and plodding. There is a lot of discovery and experimentation, and this takes time. Early blocking rehearsals can get very tedious, as the actors and director search for just the right movement or gesture that will fit comfortably with the lines of dialogue and with the motivation of the characters.

Sometimes there are conflicts. On the one hand there is blocking that is called for in the script, such as entering through a door or opening a window. And on the other hand, there is spontaneous blocking that is motivated by how an actor "feels." Invariably this will prompt great discussions about specific motivation. Sometimes a director will try different approaches to a specific "moment" for a day or so, before a decision is made. Sometimes a line will be cut or another one added in an effort to help the situation. Whatever the problem, solution or compromise, it is the nature of rehearsals and all in a day's work.

All blocking is recorded in the stage manager's master script so that the next time that the scene is rehearsed everyone's movements can be checked for accuracy. The actors also write down their blocking in their own scripts. Blocking is always written in pencil, because blocking always changes. I have never been involved with a Show where the blocking that was worked out in the first week of rehearsals bore any resemblance to the final blocking that was performed on opening night.

The early music rehearsals, as you can well imagine, are also slow and meticulous. Each song is played by rehearsal pianists and broken down into vocal parts. Each singer listens to his or her part, sings it, listens to it, tapes it on a cassette tape recorder, and sings it again. Each vocal part for each singer is taught the same way. This process is repeated, daily, until every part in every song is committed to memory. Some performers pick up music instantaneously. Others do not. The cassette recordings are an aid for the homework of those who do not.

Dance rehearsals follow the same pattern—step by step, movement by movement, learn and review, learn and review. The choreographer or the dance captain will demonstrate each sequence in front of mirrors as the dancers follow. Step by step, over and over again, the movement is repeated by counts: 1-2-3-4-5-6-7-8, until large sections or even whole dance numbers are learned—and then it is done to the music! It's a long exhausting process. Dancers probably sweat more than anyone in the theatre.

While some dancers are learning one routine others may be rehearsing in small groups going over routines that have already been taught. Repetition is key. As the assistant to the choreographer, the dance captain is in charge of seeing to it that the choreography is done correctly when the choreographer is not present—both during rehearsals and after the Show has opened. The dance captain records all of the movement on paper and, along with the PSM, will have the future obligation of maintaining the Show exactly the way it was directed and choreographed.

When the chorus is pretty much on their own, and the dialogue sequences have been blocked in a rough fashion, the musical director and choreographer will steal some time to work with the principals on their musical numbers. If there is a star in the Show it is not uncommon that he or she has already worked a little on some or all of the musical numbers ahead of time, before regular rehearsals started—possibly even before most of the cast was chosen. The director will be on hand for these rehearsals, making sure that the Show's style is consistent and that characterizations follow through from dialogue to musical numbers and from musical numbers to dialogue. He will also spend time in the chorus rehearsals to check on their progress. Even though there are three people "directing" this musical, it is the director who will see to it that everything is unified. There should only be one style, one approach and one vision on a Show, if there is more, it can be disjointed and chaotic.

When almost all of the dialogue, music and dance routines have been committed to memory a run-through of the Show is scheduled so that everyone can get a sense of the Show's continuity, flow, and of how much work still needs to be done. Actually, it is more aptly called a "stumble-through" or a "work-through" because there are bound to be a multitude of mistakes and stops and starts. Everything is still quite rough at this point. The choreography will be unsteady; actors may still be unsure of lines which will require some prompting; and, more than likely, most of the harmony for probably every song will have gone right out the window as if it had never been learned.

But from this initial run-through much is determined. The director will get an overall picture of what needs more work and it usually involves the whole Show. At the end of this run-through there are usually a lot of jokes and a few good-natured, sarcastic remarks about certain performances or songs and everyone usually goes home realizing the work that needs to be done.

For the next week or so, the rehearsal schedule is broken down into the running of scenes, from beginning to end, with the director taking notes on the good points and the bad points. Quite often the rehearsal may come to a complete halt so that a problem can be ironed out. During the note session after the running of each scene, the director addresses things like character development, line deliveries, timing, blocking adjustments, gestures and vocal volume. The musical director and choreographer will give similar notes. After all of the problems have been discussed and fixed, then the scene is run again, with all of the adjustments, to see how it looks. New notes are taken, on the same or different problems, and the process is repeated until, hopefully, eventually there are no more notes and no more problems.

Each time a scene is run it gets tighter. The characters become real people and begin to relate to each other as real people do. The dialogue becomes much like ordinary conversation. The choreography becomes more fluid, almost second nature. Songs begin to sound inspired. All of the movement on the stage begins to look casual and effortless not contrived or staged.

Each day is spent on one or more scenes. After several days of scene work entire acts are run and worked in the same way. Dance brush-ups and music refreshers are happening simultaneously in other rooms, or first thing in the morning, or as the last thing at the end of the day. Every effort is made to keep everyone active and to address all of the weak spots in the Show.

A performer who is not involved with a rehearsal in progress can usually be found running lines or lyrics or dance steps with a fellow performer in some hallway or restroom. If a Show has never been produced before then there will undoubtedly be dialogue rewrites or cuts or whole scenes may be dropped or added. If a song is cut, or a new one added, then choreography will change. There may even be some cast changes. The Show may be beefed up and the cast may grow, or just the reverse, some characters may be written out or the musical numbers may be scaled down to save money, hence eliminating one or more chorus members. Sometimes performers—even stars, are simply let go for "artistic differences."

Usually, during these shaping rehearsals, some "problem" costumes are made available for actors to use. They may be costumes that are part of a "quick change" that must be timed, or difficult to work in, requiring extra rehearsal time. In the meantime, final fittings are taking place for the other costumes, and the costume designer and her staff are busy cutting, dying, and sewing their nimble little fingers off in order to get everything finished on time. One of the biggest costume shops in New York is located in the same 890 Studio building where rehearsals take place, making it very easy for on-the-fly costume fittings during rehearsals.

Props have been added and cut as changes are made. If something is needed the stage manager will connect with the prop person and the added item is built or acquired and delivered to the studio as soon as possible. The sooner an actor can get used to handling her props, the more comfortable she will be with them.

Based on conversations with the director and the scenic designer, and a few visits to rehearsal, the lighting designer will finish designing the lights for the Show and place the order of equipment that must be rented from a lighting company. The LD can do little else until it is time to move into the theater where a truck will be waiting, filled with the required equipment in boxes or crates ready to be unloaded. If a new scene has been added or cut requiring adjustments in the set design, the PSM notifies the set designer immediately.   It may mean saving or spending money, or halting or adjusting work that is presently being done in the scene shop where the set is being built.

By the end of the third or fourth week of rehearsals the Show has taken on the general shape that it will probably have on opening night (barring major difficulties). At this time the producer returns to the studio to watch run-throughs. All through this rehearsal time, the set and lights are being loaded into the theater so that when rehearsals are at the stage of run-throughs, final arrangements are made to move into the theater for the addition of the technical elements. Publicity is fully underway.

When rehearsals are finished at the studios, everything must be moved out. All of the props, as well as the stage managers' supplies and equipment, are loaded onto a truck and transported to the theater. Then, all of the tape is pulled up from the floors and the studios are ready to be cleaned and rented to the next Show.

Rehearsals: Tech

It is time to pull all of the elements of the Show together at the theatre; scenery, lighting, costumes, make-up, hair, orchestra, singing, dancing and acting. It is almost like a giant, life-size puzzle coming into view for the fist time. The difference is that each piece has been made by different people so that there will need to be a good deal of sculpting and polishing to make all the pieces fit.

This time is often called "tech week," or "tech period," because a greater amount of time will be spent on the introduction of all of the technical elements. And rehearsal time must be spent working out the technical details—just like singing, dancing and acting. Lighting designers need to set lighting levels and lighting cues. Scenic designers need to set cues regarding the movement of the scenery. And the stage crew and wardrobe crew must set and rehearse cues involving the movement of props, scenery and costumes.

It all began, as we have said, with the load-in when the set, lighting equipment, props and costumes arrived at the theater several weeks previously. When the actors arrive at the theatre they will be rehearsing, in most cases, on still unfinished sets under partially focused lights with props still being built or painted. These rehearsals progress at a snail's pace. Everything is getting "finished" simultaneously.

Generally, during tech time, crew work on the set and lights happens in the mornings from 8 am till noon. The cast arrives at noon and warms up or gets notes from the director and, when the crew returns from lunch, the rehearsals onstage begin. As the performers rehearse each scene the scenic designer sets the scenic elements as intended. Some spacing in the musical numbers may be changed because of sight lines or traffic patterns. Through it all, the lighting designer "lights" the Show. He decides which lights are needed for each scene and how bright they should be to illuminate what must be seen. And the director is always watching and listening and giving his approval or suggestions for changes or alterations.

When each light "cue" is established it is recorded on the computer and the PSM makes a note of when the cue will happen in his master production script. During the performance, the PSM will "call" each cue (sometimes verbally, sometimes with a cue light) so that all of the changes of light, as well as the shifts in scenery, will occur routinely for every performance. These cues are called over a headset to an electrician who operates the dimmer board or to the carpenters who move the scenery on the stage. There is a great deal of effort involved in establishing just the right timing for every cue. This is what makes tech rehearsals take such a long time. Each set change or light cue is run over and over again until all the action on stage runs smoothly and according to plan.

This process is a strain on the actors who must keep

their concentration at all times. But remember the actors are polishing their performances as well. Everything is getting fine-tuned. Gradually each scene and scene change begins to run smoother and smoother and there is less and less stopping and starting.

As the days slog by, the Show is taking shape. Actors and crew are working out the backstage choreography so that everyone knows where to be at what time so no one either gets hurt or misses his or her cue. The morning crew work is drawing to an end. Now the backstage area and the basement and the stairwells are being tidied up and cleared of all debris so that people can walk around with ease.

Dress rehearsals begin a few days prior to the first public performances or "previews." Costumes are being worn, as well as make-up and wigs. These elements need to be addressed in terms of comfort and appropriateness. Aside from preliminary fitting, this may be the first time most have ever seen any of these elements except in terms of design drawings. Quick changes need to be worked out. Incidental music or dialogue may need to be added to cover difficult changes.

The director is still taking notes to make each performance even better. There are vocal notes and dance notes and lighting notes and set notes and costume notes. Every night after every rehearsal there is a note session to discuss these mistakes or changes. Every morning the notes are addressed in specific work calls or rehearsals. By the afternoon of each day the Show is run from beginning to end. Then there is a dinner break followed by another run-through.

Then there is a "final dress" performance to which the cast and crew are permitted to invite friends to see the Show. The theater is cleaned including the removal of all of the production desks that have been built over the seats in the theater. The PSM begins calling the Show from backstage or from a booth out front. The electricians move to the booth to control the lights. Programs have arrived from the printers. Stars have been making TV appearances to "sell" the Show. Ads are running in daily newspapers. The Show has become a Show and the excitement is building. This final dress rehearsal is the only time anyone ever really gets into a Broadway Show for free and since the audience is filled with family and friends this is one of the best Shows to see. The energy is up. The audience reactions are great. Applause and laughter is plentiful. This Show is like a special gift to the cast and it makes everyone feel great.

Although the length of a Show's tech period is predetermined for scheduling purposes, a producer will usually add more tech rehearsals to the schedule if there are still problems to be worked out. This addition of extra rehearsals will probably push back preview performance and maybe even opening night. Some opening nights have been postponed a month or more if a Show still needed work. But once everything is ready then preview performances begin.

Previews

Previews are the performances in front of a paying audience prior to the official opening night. The number of preview performances can vary anywhere from two or three individual performances (Off-Broadway) to a month or more, eight times a week. The latter example is characteristic of a Broadway Show that previews in New York at the theater where it will open. Sometimes a Broadway Show will preview out of town in one or more different cities before moving into New York. A Show that previews out of town is said to be doing "out of town tryouts." Some Shows do a combination of out-of-town and in-town previews.

Preview performances serve three important functions. First, they provide the director and the producer with essential audience feedback. Nothing is more crucial to a Show than how the audience will react. An audience can mold the final shape of a Show simply by reacting or not reacting to a preview.

Second, if a Show is in good shape at the time of previews, then the preview audience can become a publicity device generating vital word of mouth advertising. Sometimes a Show can generate a respectable advance sale of tickets by this word of mouth promotion.

If the Show is still in bad shape, either from technical problems or script and performance problems, then the third reason for previews becomes a financial one. It's very simple—ticket-buying audiences pay bills! Salaries, the money needed to fix a faulty set, new props or new costumes don't grow on trees. And although a wisely budgeted Show has a built in reserve for emergencies, very often it is just not enough to offset the real expenses. So the preview audience can help ease these extra costs and allow time to fix the problems.

If a Show can sell out its preview performances then it can usually keep up with its weekly running costs and bide the time until the Show is ready for opening night. A past Broadway Show called *Lolita* is an example. This non-musical previewed in New York for almost five weeks, which followed several weeks of out of town tryouts in Boston. It was playing to sold-out audiences who were being drawn to the Show because of its sensational subject matter. Even though the New York critics panned the Show on opening night, and it closed within two weeks, it had made a considerable amount of money in previews which eased its financial losses.

The first preview performance is like a miniature opening night. For the first time since the first read-through the Show is getting spontaneous reactions again—different from the final dress when friends laughed and applauded everything. Some of these spontaneous reactions are favorable and some not so favorable. The director watches and listens. The producer watches and listens. The actors continue to get notes the following afternoon when fix-up rehearsals are scheduled. Dialogue, music and choreography may be changed or added. Light levels may be adjusted and set pieces may be altered or reworked during morning work calls. Anything and everything is done to make the Show work—and work well. Every performance is observed and analyzed with all the creative genius that can be mustered. In extreme cases even outside help, in the form of an associate director or choreographer, is brought in to try new ideas—though this will usually happen earlier in the process.

Then, when the producer and the director decide that the Show is ready, everything is set. Rehearsals stop. All of the sweat and effort, all of the changes and adjustments, all of the notes and debates, all of the talent and genius, and all of the hopes and dreams of the entire cast rest on one performance—opening night! Why is opening night so special—since audiences have already been seeing the Show? Because opening night is when the critics write their reviews and publish them for the morning papers. And the reviews decide if the Show will run or close.

Opening Night

Nothing compares. There is so much adrenaline flowing, so much energy and electricity, affecting so many people, that it defies description. Suffice it to say, it is probably the most exciting, inspiring and gratifying performance ever given by a company of actors; ever taken part in by a single actor; or ever observed by an audience.

No matter what Show; no matter how many opening nights one has seen or taken part in; no matter whether the Show is good or bad, a hit or a flop—nothing compares to Opening Night.

Although the Show will probably settle into its final "look" during preview performances, there still may be a last minute rehearsal called, on the day of opening, to make one final adjustment in blocking or set change or lighting sequence. Some say that by this time it is best to leave well enough alone, that there is little to be accomplished in last minute attempts to make a Show better. But theatre people are committed to always trying to do their best. And if a producer, director or choreographer sees one small detail that he or she feels could be more perfect, then every effort will be made.

After the last minute rehearsals, the cast will take a long dinner break so that they can take a well deserved deep breath before the important performance. And even if they don't actually eat, they will rest and contemplate what the evening has in store. Meanwhile, the stage crew is putting the stage and scenery in order, checking everything one more time and fixing everything that may need attention. They may even rehearse a set change or a scenery shift on their own in order to work out the smoothness or timing it takes to accomplish the move.

Flowers and telegrams are being delivered to the theatre all day long. Parents and friends may be arriving from out of town. A red carpet may be rolled out in front of the theatre as a festive way to welcome dignitaries, famous people and critics when they arrive in their limousines. One can easily tell when there is an opening night on Broadway by the numbers of limousines that line both sides of the street in front of the theater—double-parked!

Curtain time for Broadway opening nights has, in recent years, been rescheduled from the regular 8 pm to a more convenient 6:30 pm. This allows more time for the TV critics who must write reviews before the 11pm news broadcast, and it also allows more time for having a cast party after the Show that won't last until the wee hours of the morning.

The cast party after the Show is a time for celebration. Its main purpose, traditionally, was to allow the cast to wait in a group for the reviews to come out, which would determine the fate of the Show. In earlier days, the party was held in an intimate setting—perhaps the producer's home or star's home, or even a small club. More recently, it has become a large party, not limited to just the cast and staff, but also including friends and family and other famous people not directly connected with the Show. Opening night parties are now held in big ballrooms or large restaurants (most notably—Sardi's) with catered meals and entertainment.

As was said, the main purpose is to wait for the reviews and to celebrate madly if they were good ones. But even if they are bad the opening night party is an opportunity to celebrate all of the time, effort, joy and tears that have gone into creating the Show, because no matter what the reviews say, theatre is an experience that is satisfying just for the process, regardless of the outcome.

The outcome. That's the big question. Will it be a hit and run for years or will it be a flop and close that very night? Unfortunately in the American theatre the answer to that question rests solely in the hands of a dozen or so men and women who hand down the verdict. They are called the critics.

The Critics

Who is this jury that will bring down the verdict? It is not the cast or staff or crew—who are the most familiar with the Show. It's not the audience who may have come from all over the world to view the opening night performance—an audience made up of dignitaries, celebrities, fellow theatre people and even ordinary citizens who may have laughed and cried, cheered and applauded and maybe even risen to their feet with bravos!

No! The audience doesn't determine the fate of a Show. Despite the money, time, energy, work, plans, desires, prayers, hopes, dreams, and talent, it is left in the hands of these dozen or so critics who have been given the unquestionable power to determine the fate of every Show.

On TV or in print, good or bad, right or wrong, correct or incorrect, inspired or impaired, it is the irrevocable judgment of the critic that prevails. Years of planning, months of hard work and buckets of boundless energy will only pay off if the jury finds in favor of the Show. The fate of thousands of talented professionals, Show after Show year after year, is determined by the opinion of a handful of men and women whose pen and/or tongues have become mightier than all of the talents of all of those professionals combined.

It used to be that all critics came to the opening night performance, and during the curtain calls rushed back to their typewriters to bang out a quickie review before a deadline for the morning edition. No longer. Not on Broadway anyway. Years ago a new procedure was initiated, allowing the first string critics (those who write for major daily New York papers or report on network TV) to attend one of the final preview performances prior to opening night. This gave them an extra day or two to write their review, which would still not be printed until the morning edition after opening night, or aired on the evening news on opening night. These reviews generally come out in time for the opening night party thereby maintaining opening night jitters and suspense. Other critics, who don't have immediate deadlines, still attend on opening night.

For Off-Broadway Shows the critics, though less in number, usually wait until opening night or after. Reviews may appear in print or on TV (a rarity for Off-Broadway) at any time over the next several days as space permits. Reviews for Off-Broadway are not guaranteed a next day printing because there is a feeling by publishers that they are not as important—unless it is an established theater or there is a big named star in the Show.

Off-Off-Broadway Shows can only pray that a critic

will come. Since there are a great deal of Shows to see in this arena, the critics become very selective in their attentions. As with Off-Broadway, the more established Showcase theaters stand a better chance of being reviewed, by at least one major newspaper, and again, if there is a star in the cast, the chances are even better. For the most part, however, those little Off-Off-Broadway Showcase productions go totally un-reviewed, which is unfortunate because a review is, in many cases, the only form of publicity a small Show can afford. (More about Off-Broadway and Off-Off-Broadway later.)

But who are these critics who can pick and choose the Shows that they will bless with a favorable review; who can have curtain times changed to accommodate their writing habits; and who rely on producers to schedule Opening Night dates so that no two opening nights occur simultaneously? These critics also receive the best seats in the house—for free, are pampered and cajoled by press agents, loved by hits and hated by flops? Who are these critics who seem to hold the entire theatrical industry hostage to the keyboards of their computers?

Well, first of all and most importantly, they are people. Yes, ordinary people just like you and me who probably love theatre and have valid opinions just like we do. Most critics are usually well read and possess an above average degree of intelligence and articulation. Some critics have actually written about theatre for many years.

In most instances, however, theatrical critics have never been an active part of the main stream of the struggling theatre world. They are writers, that is to say, journalists, who are being paid for what they do. Their jobs do not depend on good seasons. Most have never been actors, directors or designers. Their opinions are based on observation and they influence the judgment of masses of people. There is a tremendous responsibility in that.

We, the audience, have been conditioned to respond

to the critic as exactly that—an audience. We forget that we too have opinions and we can express them and possibly also have an influence on the theatre that we care about. How many times have you read a bad review of a Show that you yourself saw and enjoyed?

We want a review to tell us about the Show so that we can decide if we will like it or not. So we read reviews to help us make decisions and there will always be a risk. The more advice a person has the better the decision will be. The best thing to do is to go to the theatre and decide for yourself. Remember, even if everyone hails the success of a Show doesn't mean you will like it.

Let your opinion be known as well. If you see a Show and you disagree with the critic's opinion, write a letter to the cast and producer of the Show to let them know what you think. If a Show is teetering on lukewarm notices, deciding to make a go of it or not, then letters of encouragement might give a Show the needed amount of incentive to stay the course. Like the 70s Broadway Show *Grease* which opposed negative reviews and answered the audience's support to become one of the longest running Shows in Broadway history.

Generally speaking, this is a simple way for anyone to take an active part in Show Business—after all, as the audience, you are a vital part of any Show. Whether you have a friend or a family member in the business or you are just an avid theatergoer, it is your business too and you have a right to choose the type of theatre that you want, not just what is "sanctioned" by others. Remember that no producer, director or company of actors sets out to do a bad Show. And I believe that there are far too many Shows that have died untimely deaths because of questionable critical opinion. Maybe this should change.

Why did I say all of this, you might ask? Why did I spend so much time talking about the critic (and maybe even risking their wrath)? The answer is quite simple. It is a burning issue with me and a great many other theatre people who want theatre to live and flourish. We don't believe that half of every Broadway season of Shows should close within weeks of opening night. No one will convince us that all of these Shows were bad and deserved this fate. If by stating my opinion (like the critics do) I can bring to light another side of the issue, and in some way encourage accountability of critics to their audiences, and maybe save even one Show from undeserved extinction, then I must do so—and hope that others will do the same.

A Flop

By definition, a "flop" is a Show that has gotten almost unanimously bad reviews. The term is used to apply to what the critics say are the worst Shows. Flops generally close on opening night and the cast has little to do about it except clear out their dressing rooms and start looking for another job.

As is the way with almost everything in theatre, there are different degrees of flops. There are the flops that close overnight and there are the flops that hang on despite the bad reviews, and try and make a go of it. How long these Shows last can depend upon how many bad vs. good reviews the Show got, how popular the subject matter is, how popular the stars are, or how much money the producer can pump into it in order to keep it going.

The decision whether to close a Show early is usually made at the opening night party or by the next afternoon. At least that is when the decision is usually made public or posted as a notice on the callboard at the theater. The producer is the person saddled with the pressure of making that decision, although he may consult his financial advisor, his general manager, the director, star or investors.

The facts must be weighed. How many bad reviews? How many good reviews? What did the New York Times

: Working in the Theatre 121

say? In many instances the decision may be made based on the answer to the last question. The New York Times review is generally regarded as the barometer for a Show's success as well as the barometer for other reviews. If a Show gets generally lukewarm to negative reviews from other critics, but the Times review is favorable, the Show may elect to stay open. On the other hand, if the consensus of opinion is moderate, with a negative Times review, then the Show will probably close very soon, if not on opening night. It has been very difficult in the past to try and buck an unfavorable Times review.

If a star or stars posses drawing power or if there is money available to keep a Show going, in hopes of building a good word-of-mouth, then the decision may be to give it a try. Shows that take these risks have days that are numbered. Usually it's just a matter of time.

Whether a Show closes on opening night or soon after, it's back to square one for everyone involved. There may be a short vacation for some actors but afterwards they simply re-type their resumes and start hitting the boards again looking for a new Show. The designers also update their portfolios and begin fielding new inquiries. The director starts reading new scripts.

Only the producer and his staff have unfinished business. They must dismantle the Show and close out all accounts before their job is through. The scenery must be stored, sold or disposed of. The rented lighting equipment must be returned. Costumes are often donated to New York costume houses or returned there if they were borrowed or rented in the first place. Some costumes as well as many props often become souvenirs for cast and crew members. Business charge accounts must be paid off, even though the Show is broke, unless bankruptcy is declared.

In general, the theater must be returned to its original condition—empty and clean, and all of the business of the company must dwindle down into folders in the closed drawer of a file cabinet. After that, the producer starts to work on his next Show hoping this time it will be a hit.

The Gamblers and the Sad Tales

There are two types of Shows that are gamblers. The first is the Show that tries to override bad reviews and attempt to make a go of it. Stories of these types of Shows are indigenous to Broadway folklore. Two famous examples from recent history are *Grease* and *The Fantasticks.*

Grease opened to lukewarm notices suggesting that the Show should close. The producers, however, decided to stay around. It was during the early 70s when the 50s nostalgia movement was becoming very popular. The producers of *Grease* (a Show about a 50s high school) decided if they could just weather the storm then perhaps the wave of the 50s movement would pick them up and carry them along. Their gamble paid off. Not only did *Grease* make a go of it, but it went on to run for eight years—a record that was previously held by *Fiddler on the Roof* and which was subsequently surpassed by *A Chorus Line* on September 29th, 1983. And *Grease* even became a vanguard for the 1950s movement. It not only was the launching pad for the careers of several of its performers (notably—John Travolta and Richard Gere) but it made commonplace the character of "the Fonz" in the hit TV series *Happy Days.*

The Fantasticks, which opened Off-Broadway in 1960, also decided, contrary to most critics, that the Show was something that audiences would want to see. And they did—for 42 years! It closed in January of 2002 at the Sullivan Street Playhouse as the longest running musical in theatre history.

Cats is another example of a Show that got negative to mixed reviews and stuck it out. It opened in 1982 and closed in September of 2000 as (at the time) the longest running Show in Broadway history. *Grease* was one of the first Broadway shows I ever saw; I had a friend who played "The Girl" in *The Fantasticks;* and I substituted on *Cats* as a follow spot operator.

Not all Shows, however, can take the gamble and come out on top. There are some Shows that are just plain terrible and should listen to the advice of the critics and of the audiences. The 1981 Broadway Show *Marlowe* is an example. This Show opened to the worst reviews that anyone could remember in ten years of Broadway history. But despite the writing on the wall, the producers found literally hundreds of thousands of dollars to keep the Show running for six weeks. They hoped to build up a good word-of-mouth but instead turned the Show into one of the biggest jokes on Broadway. I know because I made my Broadway debut with this Show as a stage manager and later as an actor when there were injuries in the cast. The decision to keep *Marlowe* open may have been well intentioned, but the desire backfired.

Then of course there are the sad tales of Broadway. These stories are about Shows that were really quite good, and in most cases wonderfully entertaining, but the producers made the decision not to go against critical opinion. They died what some feel were premature untimely deaths. A Show I worked on in 2002, *Sweet Smell of Success,* starring John Lithgow was one such Show. We thought we had a unique and entertaining Show on our hands, the audiences gave us standing ovations nearly every night of previews and word of mouth seemed great. But we were shocked by the negativity of the reviews with some critics going so far as to mention how "bad" our Show was in reviews for subsequent Shows. It was almost like a ruthless vendetta against our Show and no one could figure out or understand why. *Sweet Smell* went on to garner several Tony Award nominations, and John Lithgow proudly took home the statue for Outstanding Actor in a Musical.

There is nothing to be done in a situation like this. Despite burning desires, complete and utter confidence of the cast and producers and the support of huge numbers of audience members, Shows like this can't stay open. The reasons are usually financial. In the world of commercial theatre where money talks, art for art's sake very rarely survives.

Sad tales of Broadway do however accomplish two things. They rally those involved to a deeper commitment to do even better work in the future. This commitment is the heart and soul of theatre and of theatre people. And secondly, it rallies these theatre people and their audiences toward challenging the state of theatrical criticism. Because no matter what sad tale we are talking about; no matter what Show closes before its time, the critic can usually be found somewhere at the root of the sadness.

A Hit

There are degrees of hits just as there are degrees of flops. Some Shows open to glowing reviews which, coupled with big name stars, keep them running for long periods of time to capacity houses. Some Shows have wonderful reviews so they last only as long as the publicity can maintain the public awareness of the Show, or as long as the original star stays with the Show. Then there are Shows where the Show itself is the reason people come. Like *Cats, Phantom of the Opera* or *Les Miserables*. These Shows are hits because of some built in appeal to large audiences who continue to buy tickets. The Show *Annie* was another example. It had a pre-disposed, built-in audience of everyone who had ever read the Sunday comics and just about every kid who could drag his or her parents to see it. There are not too many Shows for kids on Broadway, so it became a hit and did a whopping business for several years, playing over 2300 performances—and it wasn't necessarily because it was a great Show. *The Lion King* has no stars. The Show is the star and it will run forever!

But, getting back to *our* hypothetical Show, let's say that the critics were kind in their comments and the Opening Night party turned into a real celebration. In fact, in some instances, the critics even raved! There were also several wonderful mentions naming several actors (one called a "triple threat" – singer, dancer, and actor), as well as our director and set designer. What will it all mean?

As far as the Show is concerned, it will keep running as long as the bills are paid. Because even if the reviews are good, people still have to buy tickets. So, only as long as the audiences keep coming, will there be weekly paychecks for everyone. If the Show runs for a long time, those salaries will probably increase along with the cost of living. Members of the cast may leave for better work or out of boredom and new cast members will replace them.

Through it all, no matter what the reviews or audiences say, a Show only runs as long as it pays for itself. Once the income from ticket sales falls below the level of weekly operating expenses, and there is little hope for the trend to reverse, then the producer will post the closing notice. The investors don't want to lose any more money than is necessary. And Shows do not stay open simply because the cast wants it that way.

Basically the director, choreographer, writer, composer and designers have finished their work and are free to go on to another Show. If their contracts involve royalties, then they will collect them for as long as the Show runs. And if they get a new Show, it is possible that they could collect royalties from both Shows at the same time.

The only member of the artistic staff that might remain with the Show is the musical director. This happens when he also functions as conductor of the orchestra. He will collect a weekly salary established by the musicians' Union, and if he has negotiated royalties into his contract he will collect those payments also.

Frequently, at the beginning of the run, and less frequently as time progresses, the artistic staff will visit and check up on the Show's condition. The director and choreographer will undoubtedly give notes on individual performances—less as time goes on—in an effort to keep the Show perfect for every new audience. As these improvements dwindle down, the job of note taking gradually falls into the hands of the production stage manager and the dance captain, who have the day to day responsibility of maintaining the Show as it was left to them.

The designers may also stop by, occasionally, to check on things. The set designer will talk to the master carpenter and prop person about repair and repainting needs. Often times, on long running shows, certain set pieces and various props may need to be rebuilt or replaced because they are handled so much that they literally wear out.

The lighting designer will talk to the master electrician about the maintenance of the lighting equipment. There are three common lighting problems that must be monitored constantly: 1) lamps burn out, 2) instruments "sag" out of focus, due to gravity and must be refocused, and 3) the heat from the instruments burns the colored gel so it must be replaced frequently. Although the lighting designer doesn't need to know about these common wear and tear problems, he may want to keep track of them.

The costume designer will obviously want to know about wear and tear on the costumes and about replacement needs when costumes wear out.

And all of the designers will want to be informed if the Show was changed in any way. Changes in casts, especially, may mean changes in costumes, lighting and even sets or props.

Everyone talks to the production stage manager about any changes, and he or she sees to it that they are implemented. The PSM is in charge of the on-going production and is responsible for the maintenance of the Show in every respect. If the Show runs for a long time, and the director no longer visits, then it is the job of the PSM to see that everything is functioning correctly and the Show has the same look and excitement as it did on opening night.

The Working Actor's Routine – 8 Shows a week

What will a typical actor's life be like, if her Show is "a hit?"

She arrives at the theater every Tuesday through Sunday and signs in on the call board prior to 7:30 pm for an 8 pm performance, or by 1:30 pm for a 2 pm matinee. These "call times" and "curtain times" are pretty traditional for all Shows, as is the Monday "dark night" which functions as the company day off. Some shows may have performances on Monday and take Sunday off. And some shows have started Tuesday night performances with a curtain time of 7:00 pm in an attempt to attract audience who would prefer an earlier evening because they have children or who may drive in from neighboring towns and like getting home earlier.

There are eight performances each week, which means two matinees, usually on Wednesday and Saturday. Sometimes there is an extra show scheduled as a benefit and everyone gets paid overtime for the extra show.

The fact that each actor must sign in no later than one half hour before curtain is not just a ritual—it's a rule. At "half hour" everyone who is actively involved with the running of the Show must be in the theater in order to be sure that everyone is still alive. It may sound ominous, but many performers and/or crew members have been involved in serious accidents on route to the theater. If someone has not signed in at half-hour, then the stage manager finds out why because an understudy might need to go on, or a new crew member may need to be found, or jobs or roles might have to be doubled up. That half-hour window before the curtain goes up gives the stage manager time to make these adjustments. After all —the Show must go on!

Another reason for assembling by half-hour is to allow time for occasional notes from the director (if he is still visiting) or from the PSM. A performer, especially a replacement, may need a little extra time on stage to check a movement or make an adjustment. Or there might need to be a hurried rehearsal for the understudy who is going on in an emergency to run through that intricate piece of choreography. In general, most performers prefer to arrive at the theater *before* half-hour so they can relax, finish one more cup of coffee and take their time with costumes and make-up.

The crew uses this pre-show time to mop the stage, set props, check to see that all the lights and sound equipment is functioning and that all of the set pieces and flying scenery are in working order.

The front-of-house staff must prepare for the deluge of audience members by setting up concession and merchandise booths, stuffing programs with announcements of any replacements in that evening's performance, and generally make sure the theatre is ready for guests to arrive.

Each week, after the Show has opened, eight hours of brush-up rehearsals may be scheduled to rehearse understudies or to make cast replacements. These rehearsals are presided over by the PSM and they usually take place on Thursday or Friday afternoons. It is always best to keep understudies fresh and sharp and these rehearsals are the only times understudies are given to keep up on the roles they may need to perform.

Replacements don't get the luxury of developing their roles like the original cast. A replacement is often cast in the Show because he or she looks and sounds like the original cast member and is expected to "fit in" to the role as it is already being portrayed. Star replacements are allowed some freedom in their roles and have even been known to change how a Show plays by their input and presence. Some stars who come in as replacements add new life to the Show and ticket sales are boosted. Some stars that come into a Show have just the opposite effect. On *Jekyll & Hyde,* when Sebastian Bach took over the leading role, ticket sales and audience reaction soared. There was great excitement surrounding his appearance, both backstage and in the audience. Six months later David Hasselhoff took over and ticket sales as well as spirits dropped. The Show closed three months later.

Actors are at the theater approximately four or five hours, four days a week, and nine or ten hours (including a long dinner break) on matinee days. Not bad. It beats a daily 9-5. The average basic weekly salary is around $2,200 (according to Actors' Equity in 2007), more for featured players and much more for stars who can make upwards of $5,000 to $10,000 or more per week. Even for the average performer it's not bad—but not great—especially if you consider the cost of living in New York. After Uncle Sam gets his hunk of every paycheck, it's hard to make the rest go very far. Only on Broadway can an actor actually save some money unless the weekly check goes to paying bills and getting out of the debt that has been incurred over the last several years just trying to get to Broadway. Remember, only about 40% of all actors are working and only 10% earn more than $50,000 per year.

Because of our Show's good reviews, the press agent will probably schedule several publicity engagements, an interview perhaps of a star or featured performer, or a photo session for a magazine article. Chances are that a TV commercial will be made to advertise the Show which is further exposure for the actors involved—and which may result in job offers to do other Shows or maybe a TV series or movie. And there may be appearances by the cast on the Tony Awards.

In no time, an actor might go from "struggling nobody" to "overnight success" and suddenly the seven, ten or even 20 years of trying and believing will have finally paid off. I watched this happen to four very talented actors who I had the pleasure of working with.

Sutton Foster was in *Les Miserables* as part of the ensemble. She left the Show to understudy the role of Millie during the out of town try-outs for *Thoroughly Modern Millie*. Somewhere along the line the person who had the lead left the Show and Sutton was called on to take over the role. She went on to get glowing reviews in New York and win a Tony Award for her performance. This was followed by starring roles in *Little Women, The Drowsy Chaperone, Young Frankenstein* and *Shrek*.

Brad Oscar (who I worked with on *Jekyll & Hyde*) had the same experience on his next Show—*The Producers*. He was understudying the role of Franz Liebkind out of town and took over when the person who had the role left the Show. He opened in New York as Franz and was nominated for a Tony Award for Featured Actor in a Musical. He even went on to replace Nathan Lane in the starring role of Max Bialystock when Nathan left the Show. He stayed with *The Producers* for seven years then joined the cast of *Spamalot*.

Also in *Jekyll & Hyde* was Kelli O'Hara. She left the Show in 2001 for a short stint in *Follies*. Then we met up again when she co-starred with John Lithgow in *Sweet Smell of Success* (also short lived, and also starring Brian d'Arcy James who is Shrek on Broadway) followed by: *Dracula, the Musical, The Light in the Piazza, The Pajama Game,* and *South Pacific.* Kelli was nominated for Tony Awards for *The Light in the Piazza, The Pajama Game* and *South Pacific.*

An ensemble member on *The Lion King*, Sophina Brown, went on to regular TV work on *Chappelle's Show, Shark,* and *Num3ers.*

All in all, very few working actors ever get rich.

These friends I have mentioned are the rare cases of the magic of theatre and the discovery of star potential. Every performer hopes for it, trains and studies for it, works hard for it, but most will never see their name on the marquee. Shows may only run for six months or six weeks, and the TV and movie deals may never come through, but at least for a while the working actor will be making new friends, nurturing valuable connections and making a weekly salary. And even while working on one Show, some actors may be out there auditioning for other things—hoping to land even bigger roles on stage or in TV or film. Some musical performers may put together club shows and perform on their own.

The main difference for a working actor is the fact that when someone asks, "what's happening?" she'll be able to answer, "I'm doing a Show!" And that satisfaction is very sweet.

The lights go to black.
The curtain comes down. There is applause.

The house lights come up.

End of Act I.

Intermission

The audience begins to chat, stretch their legs, and consult their program.

Some visit the lounge, some walk outside for a cigarette.

Others indulge in a snack, a drink or a souvenir in the lobby.

In the dressing rooms the cast is wiping sweat off their faces, changing into their second act costumes and touching up their hair and make-up. They can catch their breath, but there is not much time.

Backstage the stagehands are changing the scenery. Some pieces are being flown in the air, while others are being set in place on the deck. Props are laid out. The dressers are busy setting up costumes in quick change areas for Act II. The crew doesn't get a break at intermission.

Out in the lobby the intermission affords the chance for anyone who hates the show to leave. This happens. Even critics have been known to walk out. But, in general, the audience members tend to chat about ACT I and share opinions with friends. If the audience is viewing a preview performance they may be making their own predictions about the success of the show. If the show has already opened and the reviews have been published then the audience may be busy agreeing or disagreeing with the critics. They may also be deciding where to go after the show for a drink.

The merchandise people are trying to interest you in a souvenir from the show: a T-shirt, a mug, a poster or refrigerator magnet. Concession people will serve you all manner of drinks—from water to bourbon on the rocks. And the ushers are busy ushering people to the restrooms and back to their seats.

Intermissions last for about fifteen minutes. There is a whirlwind of activity. Some shows don't have any intermission, and a few shows have two.

The Actors and orchestra are called to their places for Act II.

The gong sounds or the lobby lights flash calling the audience to their seats.

The house lights dim to half, and then out.

The curtain goes up.

Lights up. . .

Act II :
Where and How

Scene 1 : WHERE IT'S AT

We have already alluded to several different types of theatre in our discussions thus far, but it has been mostly in general terms. It's time to get a little more specific. Although the people the process and the business of the theatre are pretty universal, there are many practical differences that distinguish the different types of theatre. To better understand where the jobs are and how theatre people go about looking for them, it is necessary to briefly characterize some of those differences.

Broadway

As far as American theatre is concerned—this is it! This is the big time. This is what everyone who loves theatre and pursues it as a career shoots for. And this is the long sought after goal that very few ever achieve. Being on Broadway means achieving success. And although shows may close, having been in a Broadway show is an achievement that will never be forgotten.

There are occasional arguments that the caliber of theatre on Broadway isn't what it used to be. That may be a matter of opinion, but Broadway is still Broadway. There are many other theaters and theatre companies, all across the country, that can boast brilliant reputations for exceptional work—but Broadway is still Broadway, and will always be synonymous with the pinnacle of theatrical success and achievement in America.

Contrary to general understanding, all Broadway theaters are not on Broadway (the street). Out of the roughly

40 Broadway theaters in New York City, only The Broadway Theater and The Winter Garden Theater and maybe the Marquis Theater (it's inside a hotel) actually have their marquee on Broadway (the street). The Palace Theater faces Times Square but it is actually on Seventh Avenue. Two more—The New Amsterdam and The Hilton Theater are on 42nd Street.

Why then are they all called Broadway theaters? Well, besides being the name of a street, the term "Broadway" describes a certain area in midtown Manhattan where all of the Broadway theaters are located. In the early days of theatre in New York there were many more theaters located *on* the famous street. When one spoke of "going to the theatre," one literally meant going to Broadway, where the theaters were located. Although most of these old theaters have either been torn down or transformed into movie houses, the term "Broadway" is still used to describe the area where the theaters are located in New York.

Geographically, the Broadway area is bounded on the north by 57th Street, on the south by 41st Street, on the east by 6th Avenue and on the west by 9th Avenue. The only Broadway theaters that are outside of this area are the theaters of Lincoln Center (The State Theater and The Vivian Beaumont Theatre) that are located at 65th Street and Columbus Avenue. The greatest concentration of theaters is in the smaller area of 44th Street to 48th Street, between 7th and 8th Avenues.

The main characteristic that sets Broadway theatre apart from any other type of theatre is its fundamental commercial nature. Other theaters and theatre companies want to make money, but usually just enough to pay the bills and go on producing. On Broadway the desire is for big bucks. If a Broadway show is not commercially successful, it will not last long on Broadway. Although artistic success is sought after and usually achieved, artistic success will never keep a Broadway show open. The show must make money and it must pay the bills. If it doesn't, it closes—good or bad.

A show is not called a Broadway show, unless it is being produced in a legitimate Broadway theater. A theater owner that wishes his theater to be considered as such, must join The League of American Theatres and Producers, and must sign contracts with all of the Broadway Unions.

The majority of legitimate Broadway theaters have between 900 and 1700 seats. The largest full-fledged Broadway theaters are the Gershwin Theater which has 1933 seats, The New Amsterdam with 1756 and The Hilton Theater with over 1800 seats. And no, Radio City Musical Hall, with over 6,000 seats, is not technically a Broadway theater even though it follows all Union rules and contracts.

Everyone who works in a Broadway theater must belong to a theatrical Union. That means actors, directors, designers, stage managers, stagehands, wardrobe, and most doormen, ushers and ticket takers. All Unions have exclusive rights in their particular fields and no one may do any work outside his or her own area. The minimum salary in 2007 for an actor on Broadway is approximately $1500 per week, more if she understudies any roles. The minimum salary for a production stage manager on a dramatic show is $1800 - $1900 per week, and on a musical it is $2500 per week. The Broadway stagehand earns an average of $1200 per week with extra for rehearsals and work calls. Stars, of course, make much more.

Most of the Broadway theaters are owned and operated by the Shubert Organization followed by the Nederlander Organization and then the Jujamcyn Organization. Disney owns The New Amsterdam and The Hilton is owned by . . . the Hiltons. These organizations may also produce Broadway shows and then must follow the contract rules of The League of American Theatres and Producers. Broadway theaters are rented to independent producers on a lease arrangement similar to that of an apartment. The only things that the theater owner provides in the agreement are the theater (with seats and work light), the box office and house staff (ushers, ticket takers and custodians) and a skeleton staff of stagehands. Everything else must be provided and paid for by the individual producer for as long as the show is running.

As with any subject in this book, it is entirely possible to write a separate book filled with information on the Broadway Theatre. But, without going into great detail about rules, regulations and procedures, I hope I've given you a "feeling" about Broadway.

The National Tour

The National Tour can best be described as the post-Broadway nationwide tour of a Broadway show. Generally only those shows that are successful on Broadway go on National Tours. There may be more than one national tour of the same show out on the road at the same time playing in different cities. And the show need not be still running on Broadway to have a national tour out on the road.

Every effort is made to make the National Tour a duplicate production of the Broadway show with only slight changes or alterations due to traveling conditions. Most of these changes occur in the technical areas, such as traveling with a good deal less lighting equipment and fewer set pieces or more portable variations. But the script is the same. And the cast is the same. So that those people all over the country are seeing a virtual reproduction of the original Broadway show.

The National Tour is usually, but not always, produced by the same producer who did the Broadway show—which guarantees a fairly accurate reproduction. There are also independent producers who produce nothing but National Tours in a profit sharing situation with the original producer.

The National Tour company performs in Broadway-type theaters in almost every major city across the country, and usually resides at each theater anywhere from two weeks to two or more months. This gives almost everyone in the country the opportunity to see a Broadway show. In major cities like San Francisco, Los Angeles, Philadelphia, Washington DC and Boston, the tour "sits" for sometimes several years.

Members of a National Tour company earn Broadway scale plus a weekly per diem of approximately $1000 for out of town expenses. The per diem pays for all of the living arrangements of each performer on the road—hotel, food, laundry, local transportation, etc. Performers can save money on the road by doubling or tripling up in hotel rooms and certainly by not eating in expensive restaurants. Some people love touring and do nothing else. In some cases they don't even have a permanent residence or rent to pay, so touring is great. Those who have New York apartments either have to pay the rent while on the road or sub-let the apartment while they are gone. I used to enjoy touring for the principal reason of eating in different restaurants and experimenting with different kinds of food. I stopped touring when I got married and had a child.

Like on Broadway, all members of the cast, staff and production crews of a National Tour must be members of their individual and respective Unions. Each show travels with a skeleton crew of stagehands (the heads of each department plus assistants) and each theater in each city must provide additional Union stagehands to round out the crew. In each city the crew arrives first and usually spends a week or more putting the show into the theatre. Very often, to avoid any down time for performances, the company has a "jump set" which is a duplicate set and allows the advance crew to begin work in the next theatre while performances are still happening in the last. The use of the jump set provides needed time for the crew to get ready for performances in each subsequent city.

The National Tour should not be confused with the pre-Broadway "tryout" tour. Although the salaries, staff, rules and operation of both tours are virtually identical, the pre-Broadway tour is just as the name implies—a tour *before* Broadway. A pre-Broadway tour may play only one or two cities and stay out for only six months, in contrast to the National Tour that plays dozens of cities and may stay out for several years.

As we have said, a pre-Broadway tour is just another way of doing preview performances prior to officially opening in New York. These shows undergo constant changes in each theater, in each city, at each performance, trying to reach perfection in order to take New York by storm and become a big hit. Some succeed, but some never even make it to New York. The phrase "closed out of town" is used to describe one that doesn't. In recent years, the number of pre-Broadway tours has diminished in favor of the more popular, less expensive New York preview. Probably one of the biggest reasons for this has nothing to do with finance or logistics. For those shows doomed to failure, it just sounds a whole lot better to be able to say: "We closed, but we closed on Broadway!"

Whether it's a National Tour of a current Broadway hit, or a pre-Broadway tour of a future one, there are theatre audiences all across the country clamoring for tickets. They want to share the excitement of Broadway in their own hometown and maybe have some effect on the shape and form of a future Broadway hit.

The Bus and Truck

The Bus and Truck Tour (sometimes called a "split week" tour) can be thought of as a scaled down version of a National Tour. It may be produced and maybe even directed by the original Broadway producer and director, but most aren't. An entirely new company is employed for the B&T, with the exception of possibly one or two holdovers from the Broadway show or a National Tour. Sets and the lighting design differ greatly from the original, but much effort is made to preserve the "Broadway-ness" of the show. Weekly salaries are less but per diems are the same, and, as the name implies, the company travels by bus and the technical elements travel in trucks. Hotel accommodations are probably on the cheaper side and the cities where the Bus and Truck tour plays are cities with great theatre interest but smaller populations. The company plays each city anywhere from four days (called a split week) to one or two weeks. Small populations do not warrant longer runs.

The staff and production crews are the same, number wise, but there may be fewer actors with some parts being trimmed and actors doubling and tripling. All Union affiliations and regulations still apply.

A Bus and Truck tour is rough on many levels. There is more traveling in less comfortable conditions compared to a National tour, along with the extra packing and unpacking of luggage. Many cast members leave after six months. But with all of its drawbacks, it is still good honest work. Actors do B&T's hoping to fill their resumes and meet producers and directors—and, of course, to work.

Off-Broadway

In almost every way, Off-Broadway is the same as Broadway except that everything is smaller, costs less and pays less.

Off-Broadway theaters are limited to 100-499 seats and cannot be located in the New York Broadway area. If the audience is limited, then of course the revenue is limited. Since the revenue is limited, and since grants and endowments do not fund commercial ventures, Off-Broadway shows are produced for as little money as possible without short-cutting all of the show's hoped for artistic goals.

Weekly salaries for Off-Broadway actors are scaled to the number of seats in the theater. Typically the salaries run about one third that of salaries on Broadway. The technical elements are only as elaborate as absolutely necessary. This includes costumes. All other expenses, including publicity, are kept at comfortable minimums. There is only a skeleton stagehand crew with commensurate salaries.

If there is such a tight hold on the purse strings of Off-Broadway, the question arises: why produce any show Off-Broadway? Well, quite simply, there is less money to lose Off-Broadway if a show fails. Although no producer wants or expects his show to fail, he is more apt to experiment and take risks Off-Broadway rather than risk hundreds of thousands (maybe millions) of dollars *on* Broadway.

Historically speaking, the Off-Broadway movement began as an alternative to Broadway both financially and, some felt, artistically. When the first Off-Broadway shows were produced as early as the 1910s, they were produced for almost nothing in small abandoned theaters, warehouses and coffeehouses. The theatre people who developed Off-Broadway saw it as a possible alternative to Broadway for artistic expression. There was a feeling that Broadway was too "formula-ized," too mass-oriented, and way too commercial. The early Off-Broadway pioneers (like The Provincetown Players and The Neighborhood Playhouse) wanted theatre with meaning and heart and soul. They wanted their audiences to come to the theater motivated by great dramatic literature and great dramatic acting, not by brassy splashy musicals with toe tapping, show-stopping chorus lines. They were willing to experiment.

In the early days of Off-Broadway, talent and the sacrificial love for the theatre were the key elements of survival. The small theaters were training grounds, indeed almost acting schools, where workshops brought forth new plays and those plays gave struggling artists a chance to stretch and grow and become great performers and possibly future stars.

It is ironic that the Off-Broadway of today has become as commercially oriented as the Broadway it was reacting against. Some feel that Off-Broadway has lost its purity because of this. Whereas in the early days, it was experimentation for art's sake, today Off-Broadway is used as a try-out arena for possible Broadway shows— experimentation of a different kind. If a producer is not 100% sure of a show, or if he is having trouble raising the capital, chances are he won't risk $5,000,000 or more on a Broadway production. Instead he might spend $250,000 or $500,000 on a miniature version of the show in an Off-Broadway theater. If it is a success, he can raise the extra money and move it to Broadway. If it is not, he has only lost $250,000 or $500,000.

Each theatrical season may tally several Off-Broadway shows making the move to Broadway. It is a small percentage. Probably the most famous conversion was *A Chorus Line,* which began at Joseph Papp's Public Theater. It was so successful on a limited budget, it immediately made the move to Broadway where it ran from 1974 to 1983 and was the longest running Broadway show until *Cats* came along.

It is sometimes hard to count the number of Off-Broadway theaters that are in existence in New York. In 2008, according to www.off-broadway.com, there are between 30 and 40. Although there are certain theaters that regularly house Off-Broadway shows, there are many that waver between Off-Broadway and Off-Off-Broadway. A theater is an Off-Broadway theatre if, and only if, an Off-Broadway show is being produced there.

Actors' Equity Association will only grant an Off-

Broadway contract to a producer if less than 499 seats are sold. Theaters or producers who qualify belong to an organization called The League of Off-Broadway Theaters and Producers.

Although all actors and stage managers must work under bona fide Equity contracts, the contract requirements for everyone else are different. Designers need not be affiliated with USA 829, although Union designers are not prohibited from working Off-Broadway. Each designer is free to negotiate his or her own contract with the producer regarding fees and possible royalties. Directors need not be members of S.S.D.&C., and they too can negotiate their salaries. The Stagehands' Union also has little jurisdiction over Off-Broadway. There may be a permanent house carpenter and house electrician employed by the theater but other crew members need not be members of I.A.T.S.E.

As Off-Broadway continues its commercial trend, it creates a certain void—an artistic void—which is what the Off-Broadway movement was meant to satisfy to begin with. In an effort to satisfy this need for an arena where art could flourish for art's sake, a new movement began in the sixties and is flourishing now. This movement is based on the same idealistic visions that Off-Broadway boasted. It is called Off-Off-Broadway.

Off-Off-Broadway

Off-Off-Broadway really began at about the same time that Off-Broadway started leaning toward commercialism. There were thousands of actors in New York and hundreds more arriving each day to seek their fame and fortune. The problem was there were only so many parts to go around. Although the New York theatre was having a heyday, commercial producers both on Broadway and Off-Broadway were not satisfying the numbers of young, eager aspirants who were flooding the boards. Hence (and in a sense for the second time) a new forum where actors could work, stretch and express themselves artistically was needed. Off-Off-Broadway gave actors, directors, writers and designers a much needed place to showcase their work in front of audiences for experience, growth and applause. They also needed a way to showcase their talents to those big time producers in hopes of a shot at one of those big time jobs. Shows in Off-Off-Broadway spaces are commonly called Showcases, which refers to the principle upon which the movement began.

In the 1960s small groups started getting together working in warehouse lofts, coffee houses and churches and even renting small theaters. They were actors and directors and usually a writer or two with a project to work on. They would produce the plays as cheaply as possible, with money out of their own pocket, hoping to get it back through ticket sales. If they did, and didn't starve in the meantime, they would do another show, and another. If they ran out of money, the group would disband. Sound familiar? It is exactly how the Off-Broadway movement started.

According to www.offoffonline.com there are roughly 80 active smaller Showcase "theaters" sprinkled all over New York. There have been as many as 500, but they come and they go. The majority of them may last a season and then are never heard from again.

As would be expected, sooner or later A.E.A. was bound to get into the act. Equity's impulse was to protect the now growing numbers of its membership who were turning toward Showcases for work and possible recognition. The possibility of exploitation loomed as a major threat in the now fast paced commercially motivated business that theatre had become—especially to the young and naive. As a result, there have developed a set of rules and regulation governing the Showcase arena.

There are two types of Showcases: "non-Equity" and "Equity approved." The non-Equity Showcases use only non-Union actors, have no protection from Equity and no rules or regulations. These shows, although few, are done in a variety of situations, and sometimes under less than adequate conditions. Many times the money that is collected is usually pocketed by the producer, none of it going to the performers. Usually very few people see these shows and even less prospective employers. The young and inexperienced performer who might work under these conditions will probably never do it a second time.

Equity's jurisdiction and the rules and regulations that were developed for the actors' protection, apply to the "Equity approved" Showcases. In order to do Equity approved Showcases with Equity actors a producer must secure a permit and sign what is known as a Showcase Code. This agreement allows the producer to use Equity actors and stage managers provided the Showcase rules and procedures are adhered to. The producer must guarantee certain basic health and safety requirements. There may not be over 99 seats sold at any performance. There is a limit on the ticket price. There must be a biography of each Equity member in a program and an asterisk after each Equity member's name on all publicity materials denoting Equity membership. There is a limit placed on rehearsal time and number of performances during the run of the show.

If a Showcase is a success and is being picked up and moved to Off-Broadway or Broadway by a new producer, or by the original Showcase producer, then the Equity members of the cast must be offered a contract to continue their roles or be paid two weeks buy-out pay (Off-Broadway conversion), or three weeks buy-out pay (Broadway conversion) at the new contract's minimum salary levels. This conversion or subsidiary rights protection is the most important rule in the Showcase agreement. The theory is that if a show is successful because of the talents of the performers, and is moved to a more lucrative setting, then the actors must be "rewarded" for their "donation" of time and talent and creative influence toward the success of the show.

In return for the actor's services, the actor receives no salary to do the Showcase, but is reimbursed for travel expenses. Any talent agent or producer or director must be given complimentary tickets and preferred seats prior to any general admission, and any other Equity members must be admitted free if there are unsold seats available.

There are no contracts on Showcases because no salaries are being paid. The Showcase Code agreement makes the "trade of services" and regulations binding. An actor can leave a Showcase at any time without giving notice. A producer can dismiss an actor the same way. Non-Equity actors may perform in Equity approved Showcases. They usually realize all of the same benefits including the seating of agents, but, technically, do not have to be reimbursed for travel expenses (they normally are) and they are not guaranteed conversion or subsidiary rights.

Some of these regulations may sound strange but keep in mind the basic premise of the Off-Off-Broadway movement: to give the performer or other artist a chance to showcase their talents in front of audiences and prospective employers, in the hopes that more and better work might result. Equity members trade off their time and talents for this opportunity. In a way, that might make the producer sound like an altruistic entrepreneur—not so. Most Showcase theaters or spaces exist on grants or subsidies and meager box office returns. The producer puts in time and energy into a show or season of shows in the hopes that something might be picked up or he can build up a large, steady, paying audience that will eventually allow him to make a profit. Until that happens, performers work for nothing. Theirs is a trade off arrangement too.

The producer of a Showcase is sometimes called an Artistic Director or Managing Director. She locates a space and, along with a few volunteer assistants, rents some chairs, reads and chooses shows to do, and often spends her own money producing them. About 1/2 of all Showcases are new scripts by struggling playwrights and/or composers. Sometimes the producer will direct as well as act in one or more shows.

Besides Equity, there are no other Unions involved in the Showcase arena. Unpaid designers and other volunteer crews help do all work on sets, costumes, lights and props. Sometimes cast members may even wield a paintbrush, but they are not required to. As a result, sets are simple, costumes are usually borrowed and it is not unlikely that a show's total budget may only be a couple thousand dollars.

Directors and choreographers that are hired get no salaries and may not even be reimbursed for travel expenses. Theirs is a trade-off arrangement as well, hoping—with no guarantee—that they may move on if their show gets noticed.

Although everything is smaller and less expensive, the rehearsal and production process is the same. A Showcase goes through the same stages, from casting to closing night, as any other show. The only real difference in the Off-Off-Broadway arena is that everyone works for love not money.

If you have watched the growth of the Off-Off-Broadway movement for any length of time, it is easy to predict that it may very well follow the same path that Off-Broadway traveled. Even now Showcases are receiving more lavish productions by producers who see a new inexpensive try-out arena for future Broadway shows. And this commercially oriented Off-Off-Broadway surge is creating yet another void. There is, in fact, a new Off-Off-Off-Broadway movement beginning (sometimes called "Scene Nights") where once again art for art's sake is trying to take root and grow. The Scene Night is another type of showcase for actors, usually organized by themselves, using scenes from established shows, no sets, no costumes and usually not even taking place in a theater. These events are geared specifically toward groups of actors getting seen by agents, casting directors, directors and producers who may hire them in the future.

Other Types of Theatre

The above discussion pretty much sums up the theatre activity in New York City but it by no means sums up all of the theatre possibilities that exist for anyone interested in a career.

There is theatre of varying kinds all across the country, sometimes sharing New York audiences, sometimes being reviewed by New York critics, sometimes sending shows to become Broadway hits and many times doing their principal casting in New York. All of these theaters have a direct influence on the New York theatre and theatre people and vice versa.

There are Resident Theatre companies, in major cities, with September through June seasons of usually 6-8 shows. There are Dinner Theaters (probably the most common local, suburban, yearlong theatre in America) that offer an evening of entertainment, combining dinner and a show. There are Summer Stock theaters and Outdoor Summer Theaters usually with summer schedules of 1-6 shows. There are theatre companies specializing in Children's Theatre, performing during the school year in grade schools, junior high schools and high schools all across the country. There are Repertory Companies where a troop of actors may perform three or more shows weekly, either at one location or sometimes on local tours. There are even some college programs that employ New York actors, directors and designers on special Guest Artist contracts.

All of these theaters and theatre companies employ thousands of actors and dozens of stage managers under a variety of Equity contracts. In a LORT company (League of

Resident Theaters), an actor earns anywhere from $500 to $820 per week and a stage manager earns anywhere from $700 to $1200 per week depending on the size of the theater. On a Dinner Theater contract, salaries are negotiated between Equity and each Dinner Theater separately. They usually end up being roughly the same as LORT, again depending on the size of the theater.

There are five different Stock Theater contracts: CORST (Council of Resident Stock Theaters), COST (Council of Stock Theaters), MSUA (Musical Stock/Unit Attraction), Outdoor Drama, and RMTA (Resident Musical Theatre Association). There are different salary structures for each Stock contract. Weekly salaries generally range from $550 to $750 for actors and $700 to $1100 for stage managers depending on the style of theatre (indoor or outdoor), whether it is a resident company or a company of "jobbers" (actors who are employed for only one show a season), or whether the show is a musical or a straight play.

TYA contracts (Theatre for Young Audiences) pay the smallest weekly salaries of any Equity contracts: approximately $420 for actors and $550 for stage managers. A lot of people not only get their Equity cards but also many times their first professional job with TYA companies.

All of the salary approximations included here were current at the end of 2007 according to Actors' Equity. One can usually estimate prevailing salaries by adding 3 - 6% for every two or three years which is the usual cost of living increase every time a contract comes up for renewal.

All of this theatre activity is governed by Equity with a separate rule book for each type of Theatre Company. Most contracts have provisions for Equity Candidate Programs which allow a certain ratio of non-Equity to Equity actors permitted to work in an Equity theater. This makes it possible for non-Equity people to eventually become Equity members.

None of this "other" theatre exists in New York City

because there would be direct conflicts with Broadway in terms of competition for audiences, paying Broadway scale salaries and the question of hiring Union stagehands, designers and directors.

Equity is the only Union that has any jurisdiction in any of these theaters or theatre companies. Stagehands, carpenters, electricians, seamstresses and prop people are generally members of the local community with talents in, or leanings toward, technical theatre. Some of these people may be on salaries, some are volunteers and many are high school or college students nurturing a theatre career.

Since the designers' Union has no jurisdiction, these theaters and theatre companies offer a valuable way for a struggling designer to gain credits and experience. Most designers are hired on a show-to-show basis and are paid fees for their work. If their work is good, they may be asked to return.

Directors also work on a show-to-show basis and the good directors are rehired frequently from season to season. Once a new director can break into this arena, he or she can build a thriving career. Directors, too, are paid a fee for their services.

Most of these theaters have permanent staffs that return from season to season.   The staff includes: the Executive Director sometimes called Managing Director; an Artistic Director who hires other directors and may direct one or more of a season's shows him/herself; a Literary Manager (if the theater reads and produces new scripts); a Technical Director (usually doubling as the Master Carpenter); a Master Electrician, a Property Master, a Sound Technician, a Costume Supervisor; plus varying assistants for each position. There is also a Business Manager, various administrative personnel, box office people, a House Manager and a maintenance and custodial staff. Many of these people are paid salaries and many start working in these theaters as unpaid volunteers hoping to move up the ladder.

The types of shows produced vary with each type of theater. Resident Theatre companies offer a season that is the most varied with a mixture of recent Broadway shows, classics, and new plays which will hopefully be discovered and move on to Broadway. Most Summer Stock theaters do seasons of established Broadway favorites with an emphasis on comedies or musicals. Some Outdoor Summer theaters do pageant type historical epics. Dinner Theaters do comedies and other light entertainment including a fair share of small musicals—but nothing heavy or too serious. All Theatre for Young Audience productions are children's theatre shows, whether written especially for children or adapted for children from existing works, using music wherever possible.

It may sound like there is a lot of theatre out there, with large audiences keeping a great number of theatre people working and eating regularly. This is not necessarily so. There is never enough work and there are never enough theaters. When you include the unknown numbers of non-Equity actors and other novice "one-time" performers, it is difficult to estimate the number of actors pursuing jobs. Not to mention stage managers, directors and designers. I heard one way of estimating the numbers that sums up the situation quite clearly: for every actor who takes a curtain call, at any given time, there are five actors, waiting to take his or her place should an accident occur as the curtain comes down. Now there aren't literally all those actors waiting in the wings, but it does give you an idea of the ratio of jobs / job holders in this business.

When I left college I went right into a Summer Stock Outdoor Drama in Ohio as a non-Union actor. I toured with a non-Union company. I got my Equity card as a stage manager in an Omaha Dinner Theatre. I also toured on a TYA contract. I did Off-Broadway and Off-Off-Broadway—onstage and backstage—all in pursuit of my theatrical career.

Scene 2 : HOW TO GET IT

There are, to be sure, many people who enter show business because they have a burning desire to be rich and famous. They yearn to be driven in limousines that pull up to the most expensive restaurants in town or to airports or harbors where planes or yachts await them for trips to glamorous foreign cities. They want to be on the "A" list. They want to be sought after for everything from autographs to command performances. They want their names up in lights. They want adulation. They want to be STARS! Unfortunately, only about 2% of all show business people achieve this goal.

Most show business people are satisfied if they are only mildly successful. To earn a good living is all that is important. They enjoy having certain freedoms and conveniences but are not desperate for status-oriented luxuries. Their goals consist of a good home, possibly a family, food on the table, an adequate pension and maybe a vacation once a year. Being "known" but not swamped by fans or "friends" is a blessing. Maybe 15% of all show business people enjoy this comfort.

The vast numbers (as much as 75-80%) may earn meager paychecks in show business, but more than likely the paychecks are very limited and may need to be supplemented occasionally by other sources of work and income. Few ever have their names up in lights. Most see Broadway shows as rarely as the non-theatre person does. They claw away at careers doing crowd scenes in movies, an occasional walk-on in a Soap Opera or Showcase after Showcase—while waiting on tables during the lunch hour. They are troupers and they remain in show business because they love it. Sure, they would love to be successful, but work is what is important— no matter how well it pays.

Then there are those for whom show business is more like a hobby than an occupation. It's something to do in the evenings after the regular 9-5 job, or while Dad takes care of the kids for a while. It's fun—and there need not be any other reason required.

Whether it is part time, partially successful or filled with fortune, it takes a lot of hard work to pursue a theatrical career. It rarely just happens. Sometimes one has to fight for it! And dig for it! And sweat for it! And starve and suffer for it! And for those who are lucky and talented enough, and want it badly enough, then maybe someday . . . There are no promises.

What follows is a look at how most theatre people typically go about pursuing their varied careers. To make the discussion as fluid as possible, we will concentrate principally on the actor. Theoretically, the pursuit of an acting career follows a certain basic general pattern for everyone even though each person's career is different. From this pattern it is easy to generalize and understand the similarities to the careers of directors, designers, stage managers, stagehands, etc.

The P & R

A Picture and Resume is essential to any actor who is serious about a career. The picture is not a snap shot or a yearbook picture or a portrait with the rest of the family. It is a color or black and white, 8 x 10, semi-gloss headshot (maybe a little shoulders too) of the actor. There shouldn't be a barn or a beach in the background. And the picture should resemble what the actor normally—actually—looks like.

Sounds clear cut and simple, right? You should see

the variety of pictures that some actors try to get away with at auditions.

The purpose of the picture is to remind all of those directors, producers and casting agents that each actor is not just a name but also a distinct face full of character. And when what you look like is as important as it is in this business, it can't be overemphasized enough just how vital it is that the picture be as accurate as possible.

Many times pictures are kept on file and from time to time a director or casting agent may consult his or her file in search of a wide eyed, smiling, cute face, with short curly hair that would be perfect for a new production of *Gypsy*. If an actor gets a call for an interview based on her pictures and shows up with long straight hair, she may be embarrassed and the director or casting agent may very well resent the waste of valuable time.

You may suggest that long straight hair can be changed into short curly hair. That's true. But few directors and casting agents are interested in how hairstyles can change. What is sought is a look that an actor already has—not one that might be conjured up. There are probably thousands of actors who could change their looks for hundreds of roles, but it is of little consequence. In this fast paced, moment to moment, sometimes ruthless business, if an actor isn't right for the part now—when the part is available—the chance may be gone.

The picture can be thought of as a calling card. It should represent the actor with the truth—not with looks that once were, or looks that might be.

The resume, typed on an 8 x 10 piece of paper (trimmed down from 81/2 x 11), is stapled or glued to the back of the picture. Neatly arranged at the top is some basic personal information including: name, email, phone(s), height, weight, hair, eye color, vocal range (for singers) and any union affiliation (A.E.A. for theatre, S.A.G. for film and A.F.T.R.A. for TV) and agent representation.

Below this information is a list of previous experience. Any Broadway credits are listed first (naturally), followed by National Tours, Off-Broadway (or any other contract work) and New York Showcases. When an actor is just starting out, his or her resume may only include college or community theatre credits. Each entry includes the name of the show, the role played, the theater and any stars or well known directors that were involved. Films, TV shows and commercials are listed separately with any descriptive information such as products, producers or networks. At the bottom, training is mentioned (including voice or acting teachers), as well as any special skills such as: speaks French and German, flies twin engine airplane, knows deaf sign language or fights bulls (you never know!).

Although every resume includes the same types of items, listed in usually the same order, including the same basic information, I have yet to see two resumes that looked alike. It doesn't matter. What does matter is the truthfulness of the information. It does no good to try and deceive someone about the 100 pounds an actor has been trying to lose, or that Off-Broadway show that an actress wanted to be cast in.

In some situations, neither a picture nor resume may be necessary. You've heard the stories about discoveries on street corners or in candy stores. These chances or breaks are part of the folklore that gives actors a secret hope. Yes, it does happen. But overnight success is the exception rather than the rule, and those that succeed this way are blessed— not always with talent—but usually with luck.

The Trades

In New York, there are two weekly newspapers (called the "trades") that tell actors where to look for many potential jobs. One is called *Backstage* (published every Thursday) and the other is called *Show Business* (published on Tuesdays). These trade papers contain as many different types of casting notices as there are theatrical opportunities—and then some. They are a great aid for actors in search of work and they can also be viewed online at their respective websites.

First and foremost in the trades are the casting notices for Broadway shows. They range from notices about auditions for new shows about to go into rehearsal; to currently running shows needing replacements in New York; or to shows mounting second and third companies for L. A., Chicago or on the road. All casting notices for major shows include basic who, what, where and when information. Those auditioning are told to prepare a monologue or that "sides" (portions of the script) will be provided with a reader, or to bring sheet music for a song (if the show is a musical). There is a cast breakdown included if it is a new show—since no one can see the script for a new show ahead of time. It is a waste of time to go to an audition if you don't fit any of the cast descriptions.

The breakdown will tell the actor if the notice is for an "Equity Principal Audition" (EPA) or an "Equity Chorus Call" (ECC), and there is usually some indication of who will be present at the audition as auditor—like the director and/or choreographer or casting director. This information is handy if an actor has worked with or knows any of these people. It might give an actor a foot in the door, or it might warn the actor to stay away if there was a bad experience. Chances are that these Equity auditions (required by agreements with producers) will take place in the Actors' Equity Audition Center on the second floor of the Equity building, 165 W. 46th Street. Actors' Equity supplies a monitor to keep things organized and running smoothly.

Besides the EPA and ECC for Broadway or Off-Broadway contract shows, there are other casting possibilities that are advertised in the trades. Some are for major out-of-town theaters that hold at least seasonal auditions in New York looking for what is presumed to be the best talent. There are theatre, film and television notices for work in Los Angeles. There are notices for Summer Stock and Tours. There are notices for trade shows and even for non-Equity shows. Night clubs, comedy clubs, cruise lines and theme parks are places where singers, dancers and comedians have a chance of building a resume as they earn a pay check. The owners of these establishments look for talent through the trades.

There may be five or ten of each type of notice in each issue of *Backstage* or *Show Business*. Each and every week, actors circle the possibilities that they feel suited for, and maybe more that are somewhat iffy, because 1) you never know, and 2) you never know until you try.

The Actors' Equity website (actorsequity.org) features a Casting Call section which is another great resource for casting and job notices. In many instances this information duplicates what is in the trades. Equity's database is searchable by region as well as type of notice and jurisdictional contract. Theatre people who are not yet members of Actors' Equity (euphemistically called Future Members) may also avail themselves of this service because many producers or directors will see non-Equity people after they have seen Equity people. The FAQ section on the site has a great deal of info about procedures and regulations.

The trades are filled with other opportunities and information too. There are some listings for jobs outside the theatre—usually office work or bar/restaurant work. There are ads for answering services, mail services, photographers, and rehearsal studios, theater rentals, voice coaches, accompanists, dance schools or instructors, acting teachers and coaches, resume typing, photo reproducing, piano tuning, yoga classes and even psychotherapy and hypnotism for the stress weary or chain smoker.

Occasionally the trades will print lists of agents and producers (with addresses) where pictures and resumes can be sent. And, likewise, lists of Resident, Summer Stock and Dinner Theaters in every state. *Backstage* and *Show Business* usually contain the same notices for Equity shows as well as reviews of shows that are running. *Backstage* also contains theatre, film and television industry news, with feature articles and advertisements just like a regular newspaper.

Both *Backstage* and *Show Business* will occasionally include a few job notices for directors, choreographers, stage managers, writers, composers, musicians as well as designers and crew people. They usually involve Showcases and possibly a Dinner Theater or Regional Theater, and, more often than not, involve non-Equity shows for very little money.

There are never any notices for Broadway shows that are looking for directors, choreographers, stage managers or designers. These shows, as well as the vast majority of Off-Broadway shows, are staffed with people that are already known to the producer. The director, stage manager or designer who uses the trades is likely to be just starting out or in need of credits on his or her resume. In responding to the staff notices, applicants are instructed to send a resume to an appropriate person and wait to be called. Interviews are scheduled with those applicants that the employer is interested in based on the resumes.

There is another trade paper, called *Variety* that should be mentioned. *Variety* is the show business almanac—with an emphasis on the business. Although it does contain a few casting notices in each issue, its major thrust is with show business news concerning film, TV (including cable), theatre and the music industry. Openings, reviews, closings, weekly grosses, legal transactions, feature stories, mergers, show biz items, top 50 film and record lists, international news, show business stock quotations and industry births and deaths are all covered in *Variety*.

No matter which trade paper is read or which notice

is pursued; whether picture and resume was requested by mail or the date and time of an audition was published, the next step is to be seen, face to face, by the people who offer the jobs.

The Audition

Whether it is an official Equity Principal Audition or any other audition it is one of those things that people commonly refer to as "a necessary evil." Most don't like them, but everyone must do them—in order to get a job.

The main, if not the only, reason for an EPA for new shows (or for replacements) is to allow the director or casting agent to look and listen to each actor for a short one to three minutes and decide whether or not they are "right" for a part. This process is called "typing-out." The casting person is almost always looking for a certain "type" and if an actor doesn't fit that "type" then he or she is "out."

It doesn't matter if the casting person is looking for character men over 55 and a young actor thinks that with a little gray hair color and a few wrinkles applied with make-up that he might be "right." It doesn't matter that the 42 year old actor really believes that she has maintained her 25 year old looks and figure and can handle the role. And it really doesn't matter if an actor has done six Broadway shows—though it might help. What does matter is what an actor looks like, talks like and possibly sings like in relation to what the casting person has in mind for the role.

Auditions are convenient for those on the auditor side of the table; the auditor can wade through all the possibilities, in a relatively short time, without having to listen to everyone read from the script or sing full songs. The down side for the auditor is the sometimes excruciating process of wading through as many as 200 possibilities for the one or two people with talent.

Auditions are necessary for actors because they

afford a chance to be seen by directors and producers and casting agents with a shot at a role now, or a chance to make an impression so that they may be remembered in the future. The negative aspects are waiting in line, slim chances and almost constant rejection.

Sometimes (especially for small theaters, out-of-town theaters, Showcases and non-Equity shows) the casting notice may have required that a picture and resume be sent prior to an audition being scheduled. This is just an extension of the "typing-out" process. It may take a few more minutes to call the actors who look interesting, but it does eliminate a lot of the sometimes boring time involved with all of the off-the-mark hopefuls who show up with stars in their eyes. I've even seen people come into the audition studio so convinced they are "right" for a part that they begin to debate the possibility. Not a good move on the actor's part (think American Idol).

The EPA is only one specific type of audition. The EPA differs from other auditions in really only two ways: First, they are required of every producer and/or theater with plans to produce an Equity contract show and must take place prior to the signing of any contracts—theoretically giving every actor an equal chance at any role. And second, the director (commonly assumed to be the person who would choose a cast) is not required to attend—especially with regard to replacement and tour auditions. Stand-ins can include producers, choreographers, casting directors and even stage managers—or a combination.

Why is the most important person that an actor should see commonly not present at an EPA? Because usually the director of a contract show (especially Broadway) has already cast the major roles and probably all of the minor roles even before the casting notice appeared in the trades. Stars are usually sought to play major roles along with established actors for minor roles. Indeed, whether a show is produced at all may depend on whether certain actors are available. This "pre-casting" happens less with Off-Broadway and other contract shows, but even so, directors will sooner turn to actors that they know rather than wait and wade through a lengthy audition process.

Why have auditions if the roles are already cast? Because there are still possibilities for understudies, replacements and subsequent casts should the show be successful or go on the road. Not to mention the fact that it doesn't hurt to be "seen" by the casting agents who ordinarily run the auditions. One never knows what other show, TV program or movie an actor might stumble upon simply by meeting a particular casting agent. The outcome of an audition is not necessarily immediate.

A quick rundown of events at the formal EPA will give you a general idea of what transpires.

On the day of an EPA, hopeful actors begin to arrive early at the location of the scheduled audition to sign up for an appointment time as much as two hours earlier than the scheduled starting time. Some will wait in a waiting area for their time slot. Others will go back home and finish waking up, having breakfast or getting "prepared." An Equity monitor will collect pictures and resumes and keep track of appointments, ushering people in to the audition studio.

Although some actors wait up to four hours before their name is called, the actual audition takes as little as one to three minutes. The process is simple and varies little from audition to audition. When the actor or actress walks into the room, the auditor will visually "type" them immediately— sometimes even before they have a chance to do their monologue or sing their song. If the actor has been "typed-out," the honest auditor will stop their monologue or song after a minimum of one minute and tell the actor that he or she is not "right" and terminate the audition. Most actors appreciate this honesty, but some foolishly think that they can change the auditor's mind. Some auditors offer to return the picture and resume to the actor (a money saver), unless the auditor is keeping a file for consideration on future shows.

In the event that an actor might be right for a role, the auditor may discuss the actor's experience, similar roles played, special talents or training. If the auditor is seriously considering the actor, a call back appointment may be scheduled, although most auditors will wait to see everyone and consider everything before any of the limited call back slots are filled.

It's all very routine, and in most cases, highly impersonal. As many as 125 - 250 actors may be seen at an average EPA, covering two or three eight hour days. Less than 3% will get a callback—which does not guarantee anything. And the rest will try again for the next show.

The audition process was designed for the vast majority of actors, none of whom are stars, and most of whom don't even have agents. They keep coming, audition after audition, and show after show despite rejection, even against their own type, hoping to get work (think American Idol again).

As a stage manager, sitting on the other side of the table, I've seen pretty much everything. Some actors walk in with chips on their shoulders and demand to be cast, and some walk in already apologizing for not being exactly what the auditor is looking for. Most take rejection very well. Some make careers out of auditioning because most auditions never result in a callback, let alone a role. For some, a specific audition may be the last straw, the final rejection, and cause them to give up their careers altogether. And for a precious few, it may just be the big break they've been waiting for.

Call Backs

Call backs are different. At a call back an actor takes a giant step from being a "type" to being a "possibility." It is during the call back that things like real talent get involved.

Along with the lucky ones who get call back appointments from the EPA's, there will be a good number of performers submitted by agents. There are also those performers who are already known to either the director or producer or writers or even the stars (who, incidentally, are usually not required to audition). Many times even the stage managers will offer certain casting suggestions. A typical call back process may last several weeks.

What happens at a call back depends upon the type of show and the special requirements of the roles that are under consideration. For a musical, the first round of call backs usually involves singing. Everyone who attends may sing a song while the creative team takes notes. If there is definite interest in someone, they may be asked to sing a song from the show or to read from the script opposite the stage manager, or opposite one of the stars that may be on hand to offer comments. Performers will only be considered and move along in the process if they can sing the roles that they are being considered for and also have possibilities in acting and dancing if required. Chorus dancers are dealt with in the Chorus Call, which we will get to in a moment.

If decisions have not been made, a second round of callbacks may be necessary and they are usually more intense. All performers will be required to do everything that is required of the role or roles for which they are being considered. They will sing again, and read or dance if they haven't already. They may even be called back a third time.

The star or stars may take a more active part now. Different actors will read different scenes together. This will be done several times with different sets of people. Singers will sing from the score, both individually and in groups. The choreographer will put groups of people through some dance steps in order to determine if they can dance the show.

It is necessary to find individual talent as well as collaborative talent. Voices need to blend for harmonies and stand out for solos. And dancers need to be . . . dancers. Whatever the director wants from each role, he will hopefully find during callbacks. He must be fully satisfied and confident or look for new people and start the process all over again. It's at a time like this that an actor who went to the EPA's and didn't get a call back, may find himself, as a second or third choice, entering the competition. You never know.

Every performer tries to read the director's mind and second-guess him as to what their chances are. If they were asked to read, maybe that means they have a shot. If they weren't, they probably blew it. If they were asked to sing several songs—maybe. If they were in and out after 16 bars—probably not. If they knew the director, and he winked—maybe. If they knew no one and no one spoke— probably not. Sometimes a director won't even know who gets cast until he makes his final decisions.

In the end, only a handful of actors are rewarded with a bona fide job offer. They will see their names in a program and can celebrate their patience and hard work. Out of the rest, there may be several that *should* have made it—just ask them. But, as we've said, talent is only part of the reason that some get hired and some do not. The strong hearted try again, and again, sometimes for the same show when it comes up for replacements, or by checking the trade papers for future possibilities. And daily, sadly, desperately, many begin their search for another career.

The Chorus Call

Chorus people (also called the Ensemble) are a separate breed of performers. They usually work in the background, singing, dancing, or just being a part of the crowd. Either by choice or by fate they are rarely ever cast in roles that have dialogue. The only time that a member of the chorus stands out in a show is when he or she is given a special dance number or song. Sometimes a member of the chorus, who is given a solo, will "steal the show." Some chorus people work hard and end up as feature performers. Most chorus people remain members of the chorus for their entire careers.

Since the main function of the chorus is to sing and dance, and there is no way to accurately gage those talents in a typical audition, the Chorus Call was established. This gives each singer and/or dancer a specialized shot at every chorus of every Broadway or Off-Broadway show. The Chorus Call is sometimes referred to as a "cattle call" because of the large number of performers who attend.

Depending upon the nature of each musical, a notice for a Chorus Call may request "singers who can dance" or "dancers who can sing," depending upon which is more important. It may also request "singer/dancers" where both talents are of equal importance. Regardless of the need, the general process followed at the Chorus Call remains the same.

At the call for singers, each person is ushered in, one by one, to sing a prepared song of their choosing (an accompanist is provided). In most cases each person is cut off after 16 bars, thanked and ushered out. Then the next person comes in, sings and leaves—and so on—all day long. There are few conversations, everyone is polite and professional, but underneath, nerves and stomachs are doing cartwheels. Only if someone is a real standout are they allowed to sing their entire song. And if there is still interest after that, the person will be asked to attend the dance call scheduled for a different time. And this process is mirrored for shows where dance is more important.

At the dance call, groups of twenty or more dancers are taught a dance routine by the choreographer or dance captain. The routine is difficult and may include steps or moves that will be a part of the show. After the dancers have learned it, step by step, and run through it once or twice, then the choreographer watches smaller groups of four to six do the routine by themselves. Those who haven't "learned it" by this time will usually leave on their own realizing that they will be cut anyway. The standouts will be asked to come back and sing (if they haven't), or to return for a major call back where all those who are being considered will sing and dance again. By process of elimination, through one or two more rigorous callbacks, the possibilities are whittled down to the most talented. Yes, what a person looks like does come into play. But with the chorus, this "typing" is done after the talent is determined, or at the very least, at the same time. Talent is really the most important criteria, and those that have it will get the jobs.

The last audition I attended, when I was still pursuing a performing career, was for the Broadway revival of *Fiddler on the Roof* starring Herschel Bernardi. I had done the show in college and figured I had a good shot at the chorus. I was on stage in the Royale (now called the Bernard B. Jacobs) Theatre with dozens of other hopefuls learning the "bottle dance." I wasn't picking it up very well (I wasn't really a dancer). And as I looked around at all the other dancers— more talented than me by far—I realized that I was not going to get this job. I left the audition and ended up working on the show as a production assistant.

Chorus Calls, like EPA's are required by Equity for all Broadway and Off-Broadway shows. Yet, unlike the EPA, where few who are auditioned get called back, let alone jobs, many chorus members for most shows are hired from the Chorus Call.

After a show has opened, and is a success, it will eventually need replacements and understudies (a chorus understudy is called a Swing). For this the producer and the choreographer will schedule a slightly different kind of Chorus Call called an Open Call. The Open Call is run exactly the same way as the Chorus Call except for one aspect: after all Equity members have been auditioned, the producer can (and most do) allow non-Equity people to audition the same way. This gives the producer a chance to find all the talent that is possible. And this is one of the very few ways that a non-Equity performer can have a shot at a "big time" show without being a member of Actors' Equity beforehand.

Agents and Managers

Agents represent. Managers handle.

Talent agents represent talent and are instrumental in getting talent in front of those people who are hiring. They serve a purpose from both ends. They act as a clearinghouse or editor regarding talent and suggest to producers, directors or casting agents only that talent that best suits what they are looking for. They also serve the interests of the talent as the person who will go out and look for casting opportunities that may be available but unknown to the talent. The agent works for the talent and earns a commission from every job the talent secures through the agent. If the talent doesn't get hired the agent doesn't earn any money.

To an actor, getting an agent is almost as important as getting a job. Actors invite agents to see them when they are working. This is why actors will do Showcases or club work—to get exposure. If an actor can land an agent, even after working for free, then the time and effort were worth it. Some actors who have an agent never get work through the agent. Some actors have more than one agent unless one agent is exclusively representing the actor. Some actors never even get seen by an agent, let alone represented.

Casting agents (sometimes called casting directors) are different. They represent the producer and director who hire them to find talent and put together a cast.

Managers "handle" the actor's careers. This is usually after the actor is established and is in a position to need a manager and can pay a manager. A manager doesn't find the work, but a manager may help negotiate contracts and perks, supervise work schedules and finances, and keep the actor in the public eye for all the right reasons. A manager may hire a press agent and a lawyer to help oversee the many facets of the actor's career. The actor pays the manager a fee.

Directors – Designers – Stage Managers – Crew

Unfortunately, there is no way to audition a director, a designer or a stage manager. Even great renderings in a designer's portfolio don't really prove anything. The only direct method to seek gainful employment, at least for directors and designers, is to already be employed so that producers can see their work live and determine potential. It's kind of a Catch-22: you need to *have* work to *get* work.

More so than with actors, it all comes down to the interview and in many cases depends a lot on personality. The choice of a director, designer or stage manager is a gamble. If the gamble pays off in the right instances, for the right people, then credibility and reputation replace resumes and even interviews, and directors, designers and stage managers will no longer need to pursue jobs—the jobs will pursue them.

For directors and designers there are no required auditions like EPA's. Resumes are sent to producers or theater companies and requests for interviews follow. But since there are few positions for each show or each Stock or Repertory season (one designer may design all the shows in one season), and many people are pursuing those positions, the interviews that result are few and far between.

Interviews that do take place are very different from auditions with actors. There is no "typing-out." A director, designer or stage manager is only called for an interview if he or she is being considered. Interviews take longer than three minutes. Designers show portfolios with photographs or renderings of their work.   Directors usually discuss methods and philosophies as well as specific approaches to particular shows.   Stage Managers are often asked about their organizational skills, problem solving abilities and technical knowledge.

Designers can show their work in an interview, and therefore be judged in a somewhat objective manner. For many directors and stage managers, talent is hard to determine, unless it can be shown in an actual working situation.   A list of credits doesn't always tell the whole story. There are no auditions. Everything is based on the interview, and many times the deciding factor will come down to someone's personality or a personal recommendation.

Stage Managers usually get work because someone who has merit recommends them—a former director or producer or even an actor. Theoretically, the EPA was meant to include a fair chance for Equity stage managers to pursue jobs as well. Those jobs are very limited, however. There are only two stage managers required on a dramatic show, and three or four required on a musical—in contrast to casts averaging 10 – 30 actors per show. And unfortunately the average stage manager faces two principal obstacles that make the pursuit of these jobs almost impossible. First, for most contract shows, the stage managers have already been hired (like the stars) even before the EPA's are scheduled. And second, casting directors who have no interest, concern or ability to interview or hire stage managers usually conduct the EPA's.

Despite these odds, a few stage managers still attend EPA's—especially early in their careers. Having attended several, I did get two auditions for shows needing assistant stage managers who could understudy. In one case, the original Off-Broadway production of *The Elephant Man,* I read for the director but was turned down. And in the second case, a Broadway show called *Strangers* with Bruce Dern and Lois Nettleton, I was "typed-out" by the casting director even though the PSM wanted me as an assistant stage manager. (This was back when more assistant stage managers could and would understudy).

Usually, if a casting notice for any show doesn't specifically mention a need for stage managers, then chances are the positions have been filled. Other ways for stage managers to be considered for jobs are to send resumes to producers and directors of upcoming shows and follow up with phone calls; or to hope that past associates or friends will recommend them when new jobs come along; or to pray that the Showcase they were working on—for free—will get picked up for a new contract production. News about upcoming shows can be found in a monthly publication called the *Theatrical Index*. This source lists all new shows being planned and the names of producers and general managers.

The importance of finding a good director and stage manager cannot be stressed enough. It may be difficult to find them. It may also be difficult to find good designers as well. That is why producers hold onto the good ones that they have found. And that is why it is difficult to break into the job market pursuing these careers, because most of the good jobs have already been taken.

Stagehands and wardrobe people are in even more of a bind when it comes to the pursuit of available jobs. There are no auditions. They hear about jobs through word of mouth. And they pursue jobs based on hustle, recommendation and perseverance. Since producers don't hire most of the crew directly, stagehands and wardrobe people seek their jobs directly from the department heads in the theaters. The jobs are limited. Very often department heads hire the same people over and over again on successive shows—many times, crew members are even relatives. And when a show closes, these crew people are unemployed and must start looking for another job. It is not

rare to find an out of work actor working as a crew person—
especially in wardrobe.

Indirect methods

Sometimes you just have to be ready for anything.
You never know when or where an opportunity for a job
might pop up. You have to be "out there" hustling and
getting seen and getting yourself known. This goes for actors
as well as directors, designers, stage managers and crew. No
one is going to hire you if you are sitting at home. And you
are not going to find out where there is work while you are
watching the soaps on TV. Networking—hanging out in the
theatre bars and hanging out with other actors or crew people
can cultivate a lead. Read the trades to find out what new
shows are coming up. Find out who the producers are. If
your friends are working . . . can they get you an interview
or even an audition? This happens all the time. I have seen
dozens of spouses and friends of cast members getting
auditions and even added to shows when replacements are
needed.

We've talked about working for free in relation to
actors—in Showcases and in clubs. Designers and directors
and stage managers, as well as crew people, all work for free
at the beginning of their careers. They meet people—while
they are getting experience and resume credits. There are
countless stories about being in the right place at the right
time; about shows that convert from workshops to contract
shows; about someone who just happens to be there, is ready
and available when that producer or director or casting agent
appears on the scene. You just never know.

You have heard the expression: "It's not what you
know, it's who you know." Being related to or knowing
someone in the business is a great way to get through doors
that otherwise might not be open. A woman in my first
Broadway show got there because she was the girlfriend of

one of the backers. I never saw her in a show before that—or since. Stagehands are notorious for hiring relatives. Sometimes this works out well. Sometimes not. But, as a way to get hired, it is definitely hard to beat. It doesn't eliminate, however, the need to be ready for the job. Education and training are vital, both in school as well as in practical applications.

However or wherever the opportunity is sought and found the goal is the same—work. Some theatre people buckle down and get busy about their careers and some hope to be discovered. Some work for years in small shows before their first big break. Others are discovered and given a leading role with no previous experience. Some design assistants move up the ladder and design on their own. Dressers move up to be wardrobe supervisors or even designers themselves. Assistant Stage Managers move up the ladder and so do stagehands—securing full-time positions after having worked in temporary situations for years. No matter what, where or how, it's all about securing jobs and the pursuit of the dream.

Scene 3 : WAITING

I t's the hardest part about a career in the theater—waiting. Waiting for the break. Those that aren't lucky or talented can sometimes wait for years. The stories of overnight success are few but real. And everyone is motivated with this hope—this dream.

Meanwhile—everyone stays prepared.

Training

No good actor will ever tell you that she is as good as she can possibly be. Actors never stop learning and perfecting their craft—nor should they. Whether it is some type of formal education, or simple daily observation, the accumulation of knowledge never stops.

There are many acting schools and studios in New York that offer programs of classes and activities in a formal setting. And there are many private acting teachers and coaches. If an actor isn't working in a particular show, which is an education in itself, then she is probably studying with an acting teacher. They may be private classes, small groups or large groups, but the educational process continues.

There are also voice teachers and dance classes. Voice teachers teach anything from basic diction and dialect to formal opera. Dance classes can range from beginners learning basic coordination, to exercise classes for physical fitness, to fencing classes, to formal dance training in jazz, modern or ballet.

Classes are held all over the city in studios, schools,

theaters and even private homes. Every day, amid the interviews and auditions, the agents and the directors, the callbacks and the rejections, performers are continuing to perfect their craft. There is a desire in the best to become even better—perhaps great. Since there is a lot of competition, an actor can't afford to be less than the best that she can possibly be.

There are workshop groups that get together and work on one or more shows. The group might include a writer and director and several actors. They may eventually put the show in front of an audience like a Showcase or they may keep it to themselves—only for the experience of working together and learning from each other. This workshop may have been designed for a playwright to work out the bugs in a new script and, when that is done, the group may disband. Or the group may develop the play for a backers' audition for potential producers or investors. No matter what the nature of the workshop, it's another way to learn and grow and hopefully get better.

It isn't always doing shows or continuing formalized training in classes. Actors can also train by making constant observations every day, in everything that they do, everywhere they go. And they file it all away. They watch people and observe situations. They talk and they listen. Someday something that they saw, or something that was said, or that was felt, will help in the development of a character.

Training never stops. In some fashion or in some degree it is an everyday ongoing process: to stretch; to grow; to get better. Even going to see shows is a form of education: to see other actor's work; to observe the technique as applied by someone else; to watch the movement, the control; to listen to the voice. The pursuit of an acting career is a continuous process. Sometimes it is said that actors are always on stage. Perhaps that is true.

And all this training can get expensive—especially

the formal training. Classes with acting or singing or dancing teachers run upwards from $30 or $50 an hour. Most performers can only take the classes when they have the extra cash. There are some schools or programs, funded by grants or contributions, that may not cost the performer anything, but it is very hard to get involved with these. Only the very good will get this opportunity and only after passing an audition. Yes, you read correctly—an audition to get into classes! It may appear that in show business only the talented have the best chance at getting better—which is another way of saying the rich get richer. It may be so. In any event, it is the talented ones who will succeed.

But everyone can observe. And everyone can go to the theatre where it doesn't always have to cost an arm and a leg. As has been mentioned, members of Equity can see any Showcase simply by showing their Equity card (provided there are unsold seats available). In many instances, producers of Broadway and Off-Broadway shows offer tickets to Equity members for free or for a reduced rate. And for most Broadway and Off-Broadway shows, tickets can be purchased for half price at a special ticket booth set up right in New York's Times Square. Shows that are in previews, or that are floundering and need to fill houses, or shows that are doing steady but not capacity business, sell tickets at this half price booth. And everyone, including the general public, can take advantage of this.

There are few classes for stage managing. Not even in college as a general rule. Stage Managing is more of an instinct than a learned talent. To get better as a stage manager, one must *be* a stage manager and exercise any inherent organizational, technical and people skills.

Directors can get college degrees in directing. But once they are out of school, there are no classes to go to. Like stage managers, they must *do* their work to get better.

Designers can "practice" designing by creating sets or lights or costumes for hypothetical shows and may be able to brush up on their artistic skills with art classes. There are a few Continuing Education classes in New York for the theatrical designer.

Crew people can learn more about carpentry or electrics or props in a variety of classes available at colleges and Continuing Education. They can learn to use the tools of their trade or get better at skills they already have.

It can be rough on the struggling theatre person, especially the ones that are new in town with no contacts, no agents, and no show to do. How can they even buy half price tickets? How can they take classes? The money keeps disappearing, instantaneously, with rent bills and phone bills and with the pictures and resumes that must be printed—not to mention food and other basic necessities. How do theatre people get by? Where does the money come from?

Survival Jobs

There may be a check every month from home. There may be a small inheritance from a favorite aunt. There may be a nest egg from all those summer and part-time jobs during college. Or there may be a loved one earning a living for two. But chances are every theatre person, at some time or another, has had to make do with a survival job.

Some people humorously call them "real jobs." They are temporary (believing the big break is just around the corner). They are late at night (leaving days free to audition or take classes). They are early in the day (leaving evenings free to do Showcases). They are jobs in department stores selling clothes; in offices typing memos; in museums hanging portraits; in restaurants waiting tables; in warehouses moving boxes; in fast food joints slinging hamburgers; in taxis listening to passenger chatter. They are three, four, or even seven days a week, and there may be more than one at a time. Some employees are allowed long lunch hours for auditioning. Some must deny their profession all together just to get the job. Some must put the theatre aside for several months or even years, in order to build up a workable bank account. Some get extended vacations or leaves of absence in order to do shows. Some make good money, others make minimum wage.

They are all called "survival jobs." They help a profession of survivors hang on, just a little longer, until that big break comes along. And, as if there wasn't enough to juggle around already and fit into a normal day, along with eating and sleeping, these survival jobs get squeezed in there too. They have to. It's all part of show business.

My own survival jobs included working at a bakery and driving the delivery truck, working at Saks Fifth Avenue hanging up the fur coats after the salespeople showed them to buyers and driving a taxi on the graveyard shift.

If you have been lucky enough to work for any length of time in theatre or on a survival job, you may qualify for unemployment. To the theatre person, unemployment is just interim money between jobs. It does not exude the same inference of destitution in the theatre world as it does in the outside world. I don't know any theatre person in any area of work who hasn't at sometime or other been on unemployment. And if you can live off the unemployment, you may then have the necessary free time to do the other things necessary to further your career.

Working in the theatre is the dream. Surviving in a part time job is the reality in more cases than not. And some survival jobs, sadly enough after several years, turn into new, fulltime careers. After all the work, all the planning, all the dreams—then what? Well, for me, if I hadn't kept working, it might have meant going back to Akron, Ohio to teach High School Math. For someone else ... who knows?

THE EPILOGUE

Why?
Maybe it teaches a moral —
maybe it even explains the reason for everything.

The Epilogue, like the Prologue,
is presented by the same cast of characters,
in the same surroundings.
It is also short and to the point,
because people have been sitting for a long time.

So... Lights resume and the Actor speaks.

So, we have come to the end of our journey. A lot has transpired. I hope that it was informative and entertaining for you. I hope I didn't overlook too much.

For me it has been a pleasure and a great cathartic experience putting it all down on paper. And, in a way, it has also been a struggle—even as much of a struggle as pursuing a theatrical career. From beginning to end it took over 25 years to finish this book. In fact, it took 40 years to *live* this book—in order to be *able* to write it. As I look back over all of the time and all of the experiences and remember all of the people, I can honestly say I would do it all again. (Well maybe not all!)

But after all is said and done there is only one other aspect of a theatrical career that we need to at least touch on. It is the hardest thing to write about because it is the hardest thing to describe. And that is: why? *Why* do we do what we do?

The answer is unique to every person who pursues a career in the theatre. From the writer to the actor to the stagehand there are many reasons—some poignant and some pathetic. But whatever the reasons, they are the reasons that brought us all together. We have left our homes and sometimes even given up our families to pursue a career in the theatre. We have starved. We have been rejected. We have trained. We have worked at menial jobs. We have succeeded and we have failed. And we have done it all because . . . *we had to*. There is just something in the heart of the theatre person that tells us to try. We have a talent or an ambition and nothing else can satisfy the desire to pursue them. We *must* do theatre. It is more than a goal—it is a dream. It is a craving. It is a need. It is an obsession. The lights and the applause and the triumph and the failure—we need it like food or water. Despite the setbacks and even failures . . . we go on. There is something inside that drives us.

If you are the parent or the spouse or cousin or friend of someone in the theatre then you may know how driven your loved one is. And you may know that you might never really truly understand the passion. Perhaps after reading this book you have come to some understanding of what we do and what theatre is all about, so that you can support and inspire your loved one to go on. We need your support and love and even your inspiration (not to mention a few dollars every now and then). We also need you to understand even if we can't explain it to you.

If someone gave you this book to help you understand, I hope it has succeeded. If you are reading this book to see what theatre is all about before embarking on a career, I hope I have told you enough—because there is so much to tell. But fear not. You will write your own book as you live your own life and pursue your own career.

If you are reading this book to determine whether you should add it to your theatre curriculum reading list, I can only hope you have determined that it has the value you are looking for. No book like this existed when I went to college—which was part of my motivation for writing it.

At any rate . . .
Thank you for joining me on this journey. It has been a pleasure to be your guide.

Go see a show!

Black out.

Thunderous applause.

Standing ovation!!

Lights up.

CURTAIN CALL

As an audience member in the theatre,
you are able to thank those who have performed for you
by clapping your hands during the curtain call.

In small groups, or one by one,
the performers will appear to take their bow.
They are finished telling their story,
singing their songs and dancing for you.

You can see their faces as they receive your praise.
Applause – it is the gift that we yearn for.

Be generous!

The People Who Helped

No one can pursue a career in the theatre without the help of others. Whether it is family or friends or various fellow professionals—there is always someone who helps or encourages along the way. I would like to take a moment here to thank several of the "major players" in my own career that gave me work or helped me take another step on my incredible journey. It is important that these people be acknowledged.

First, for me, it all started when I informed my family that instead of teaching Math in Ohio, I was going to New

York to seek my fame and fortune. Though they may not have been thrilled with the idea, they did not stand in my way. And for this, I am eternally thankful.

I have since lost my Mother and Father. But they were both around to see me get to Broadway. For this I am also thankful. And my brother and two sisters (and nieces and nephews) are still with me and are able to read this book. It means a great deal to be able to share my crazy exciting life with them, especially with my son who lived through most of these experiences with me as he grew up.

Way back in High School there was Tom LeFevre who in 1967 cast me in *The Importance of Being Earnest.* This was my first role and I was nervous as hell; knees shaking every show. This led to *H.M.S. Pinafore,* our High School Senior Musical, directed by Mrs. Sawan. And then the role of Demetrius in a community theatre production of *A Midsummer Night's Dream* directed by Thomas Spalding. I was bitten by the bug.

Not enough can be said for the Theatre Department faculty at Kent State University where I was a student from 1968-1974: Dr. Earle E. Curtis, Dr. William Zucchero, Dr. Bedford Thurman, Dr. Louis Erdmann, Dr. Jim Bob Stephenson, Dr. Alan Benson, Duane Reed, and Daniel Hannon. Even as I was pursuing an undergraduate Math degree, they cast me in shows, let me work backstage, let me direct, stage manage, design scenery and do publicity as I worked on over 40 shows and developed my skills, my appreciation and my love for the theatre. I was even permitted to enter the Graduate School in theatre because of all of my practical experience. None of these men are still there now; most have gone to that great theater in the sky, but their legacy lives on as does my appreciation.

As I was leaving KSU, I auditioned and was cast in a Summer Stock Outdoor Drama called *Tecumseh!* – thanks to Richard Nichols for my first professional job. I followed this (and some of the cast) to Ramapo College in New Jersey (on my way to New York) where I appeared as Banquo in *That Scottish Play* directed by Nick Rinaldi—who was the stage manager on *Tecumseh!* This was a great time.

Thanks to Richard Kuss who gave me my first (unpaid) job in New York in 1974 as technical director/designer at The American Theatre Company.

And thanks to Yvonne Ghareeb for my first *paid* job in New York which was actually a 1975 non-Equity tour of *1776* produced by the Continental Theater Company.

Jo Jackson hired me as the tour/stage manager (as well as the driver) for a tour in 1977 with Voices Inc. While on tour in Omaha, I fell in love with someone and returned when the tour was finished to live for a year and work in a local Dinner Theatre—which is where I got my Actors' Equity Union Card.

Back in New York, I worked at the Actors Studio in 1980 where I was Alisa Adler's assistant stage manager on a show called *Hillbilly Women* directed by Arthur Penn. The following year, when I pursued a stage manager job on the Broadway show *Marlowe,* I was hired as assistant stage manager after I suggested Alisa for the PSM position.

Two years later Jim Pentecost gave me a foot up as a production assistant on the original *La Cage aux Folles* when they were mounting their L.A. production. This turned into a job as a substitute stage manager on the Broadway production. While there, I befriended the wardrobe supervisor, Gayle Patton, who hired me as a dresser leading to my membership in the Wardrobe Union.

Gayle's assistant Irene Bunis later recommended me as a dresser on *Me and My Girl* and it was during this period that I met Kevin Woodworth who suggested my name for a tour with Harry Belafonte. I spent nine incredible months as his wardrobe supervisor and personal dresser traveling to several states as well as France, Italy, Spain and Zimbabwe.

Back on *La Cage* I also met Miles Ambrose, a

stagehand, who told me about the Local #1 Stagehand Apprentice test as a way to get into the Union. I took it, along with 700 others, and ranked 16th. When I was on tour with Harry Belafonte I got the call for my Stagehand Apprenticeship to begin. I was posted at the CBS carpenter shop for 2 years, and so, as a Local #1 Stagehand, I began the last and longest leg of my varied career.

While at CBS in 1990 Local #1 stagehands went on strike, and while walking the picket line at 3 am I met Mark Dignam. He was a carpenter on *The Phantom of the Opera* and he introduced me to the House Carpenter, George Rebentisch. This was a major turning point in my career because from this point on—for the next 16 years—I was hardly ever out of work. Thank you Mark!

I spent six of those years as a sub on *Phantom*. I continued to work in the carpentry department. I even ran a follow spot a couple of times. And the House Propman hired me as a sub in props as well as an electrician for five seasons of *Sesame Street*.

It was also on *Phantom* that I met Tim Abel who was the Production Propman. He hired me on *Phantom* as a sub, as well as on other shows he supervised: I spent a year and a half on *Les Miserables*; an all too short month on *Sweet Smell of Success* before the show closed; and in between, a couple of weeks each on *Swan Lake, Seussical* and *Oklahoma* doing prop shopping.

Tim's assistant on *Phantom* was Victor Amerling who went on to head the prop department on *The Lion King* and who gave me work whenever I was "between jobs." I worked at the New Amsterdam Theater, off and on, from the time it re-opened in 1997 after its extensive reconstruction under Disney management: first with the Gala Production of *King David;* followed by the World Premiere of the Disney movie *Hercules;* and then *The Lion King* which opened in November of that year. In 2002 I replaced a retiring crew member and became a regular member of the *The Lion King* prop crew and in 2006 fell and injured myself. I am retired now with a disabling neck injury. My son continued our theatre lineage as an usher at the New Amsterdam Theater.

So these were people who stand out amongst the hundreds I have either worked for, or with, in my theatrical career—and who were responsible for steps and "breaks" along my journey. These people where instrumental in either hiring me or leading me to other people who hired me. They gave me the opportunities to do what I do and, in a way, helped to make this book possible. So it is appropriate to acknowledge them.

And, yes, after all the years and all the shows, I did run into unprofessional and unethical people too. For those of you who are just entering the business, you should be aware that the theatre community is filled with people with a wide range of egos—it's the nature of the business. Tread lightly and watch your back!

It has been an amazing journey filled with equal parts of hard work and exceptional rewards—and fun! I would change very little of it. And I'd like to say to everyone that I have worked with: writers, actors, directors, producers, stage managers, musicians, designers, dressers, stagehands and ushers—"thanks for the memories."

Special Thanks

To finish this enterprise I would like to express my gratitude to all of the friends, relatives and associates who have helped with this book. Special thanks to Ric, Eleanore and Margaret.

In particular I would like to thank my sister Jean and my aunt Francie who went above and beyond. And much love and thanks to my wife, Cecile and son, Alex.

And many thanks to one of my oldest friends in the business, Rob Hamilton, for his perfect illustrations.

GLOSSARY
Some Theatre Terms

—— A ——

ACT
1) The thing actors do.
2) Subdivision between sections of a play. A short play is a "One-Act"; a play with one or more intermissions has two or three Acts, etc.

ACTING AREA
The area onstage where the actors move in view of the audience.

ACTOR
A term applied to either male or female performers who speak dialogue in plays or musicals.

ACTORS' EQUITY ASSOCIATION (A.E.A.)
The Union for Actors formed in 1913 which represents more than 45,000 Actors and Stage Managers in the United States. "Equity" negotiates wages and working conditions and provides a wide range of benefits, including health and pension plans, for its members.

ADAPTOR
A connector which allows two or more electrical devices to be connected to a single power outlet.

AD LIB
The improvisation of words or stage business by an actor to cover a missed entrance by another Actor or when lines are forgotten or when the normal progress of the play is disturbed by such things as unexpected blackouts, scenery malfunctions, cell phone ringing, etc.

AMPITHEATRE
A large outdoor theater with tiers of seats or stadium type benches. Similar to Ancient Greek stages. Sometimes the stage area is covered.

ANGEL
An individual or company which contributes monetarily (and sometimes anonymously) to the financial investment of a show.

ANTI-RAKE
The remedy of modifying furniture, props or equipment so that they can stand level on a raked stage. Usually accomplished by shortening the upstage portion of the furniture. Can also be accomplished by building a small anti-rake platform for items to sit on. See also RAKED STAGE.

APRON
Section of the stage which projects towards or into the auditorium. In proscenium theaters, the part of the stage in front of the house curtain, or in front of the proscenium arch.

ARBOR
In a counterweight flying system, the receiver into which the heavy steel weights are placed.

ARENA
Form of stage where the audience members are seated on at least two (normally three, or all four) sides of the acting area. See also THRUST.

ASIDE
Lines spoken by an actor to the audience and not intended to be overheard by other characters on-stage.

ASSISTANT STAGE MANAGER (ASM)
A member of the Stage Management team with responsibilities that may include collecting valuables, lighting actors exits, and handling house seat orders (among other things).

AUDITION
A try-out where an actor's skills are judged by their doing a monologue, reading from the script, singing and/or dancing. Usually overseen by a director, choreographer, musical director or casting director.

AUDITORIUM
The part of the theatre where the audience sits during the performance. Sometimes known as "the house." Ushers, concession and merchandise people can be found here assisting patrons.

AUTOMATION
Making things happen automatically. Usually refers to the movement of large heavy pieces of scenery by electrically operated cable winches or chain motors. Also can refer to automated light or sound consoles where groups of lighting instruments or sound equipment are operated by computer control.

BACKDROP
A painted or black cloth hung behind the acting area to hide the backstage and to mark the back of the area in which acting takes place.

BACKFLAP
A type of hinge frequently used in scenery construction.

BACKING
1) A scenic piece used as a background behind an opening in the set (window, door etc.) which acts as scenery or hides the areas beyond.
2) The money invested by a backer in a commercial theatre production.

BACKLIGHT
Light coming from upstage, behind scenery or actors, to separate them from the background

BACKSTAGE
The parts of the stage which are out of the audiences' sight. Includes left and right wings where scenery and props may be stored, as well as any dressing room, basement or fly floor areas.

BACK-UP
An extra one of anything: furniture, prop, lighting instrument or control console, which provides a resource for a damaged or malfunctioning item on a moment's notice.

BALCONY
The upper level in the auditorium.

BALCONY RAIL
The railing in front of the balcony. Also refers to a hanging position for lighting equipment located on front of the balcony face.

BALLYHOO
Swinging a follow spot beam around in a figure-eight pattern.

BARN DOOR
A rotate-able attachment consisting of two or four metal flaps which is fixed to the front of a lighting instrument and manipulated to reduce the spread of the light beam in one or more directions.

BATTENS
1) A length of wood or steel at the top and bottom of a cloth drop. A Sandwich batten is comprised of two flat pieces of wood screwed together with the edge of the cloth between
2) Wood used for joining flats together for support.
3) Term interchangeable with PIPE on which scenery or lighting equipment is suspended.

BELT PACK
Part of the communication system in a theatre, the Belt pack contains the controls for the HEADSET worn by crew members.

BLOCK AND FALL
A pulley on a short length of rope used to diffuse the weight of a working rope, or to suspend a single item in storage.

BLACK BOX
A kind of studio theatre where the audience and actors are in a large room, surrounded by black walls or curtains.

BLACKOUT
The complete absence of light on stage. Used for dramatic emphasis or to mark a change in scenes or in time. Theater Exit signs and other emergency lighting remain on, as do blue backstage work lights.

BLACKS
1) Any permanent or temporary black drapes used for masking technical areas.
2) Black clothing worn by the backstage crew or stage management during productions.

BLACKWRAP
Trade name for thin black pliable aluminum sheeting which is used to temporarily mask light coming out of a lighting instrument, or to control spill. A self-adhesive tape version is also available.

BLOCK
1) To map out and coordinate the movement of the actors onstage. ("Let's block Scene 2.")
2) Frame in which one or more pulley wheels (sheaves) are mounted.

BLOCKING
The movement of the actors during the play, recorded by stage management in the production script.

BLUES
Blue lights (commonly clip lights) used backstage in a performance situation so that actors and crew can work and move in the dark.

BO'SUN'S CHAIR
A small seat or cradle hung on a rope over a pulley whereby a technician may be hoisted to work up high at an otherwise inaccessible position.

BOARD
The main control console for sound or stage lighting. Usually a computer but in small theaters may be manual. The operator is said to be "on the board."

BOOK
1) Alternative term for the script or the prompt copy. (See Prompt Book.)
2) The dialogue part of a musical show.
3) To arrange the services of actors and musicians.

BOOK FLAT
Two-fold piece of scenery. Book flats are free-standing when angled open, allowing quick setting and compact storage. "Booking" describes the action of opening or closing a book flat.

BOOM
1) Vertical steel pole on which can be mounted lighting instruments. Often used for side-lighting etc. Booms have a steel base plate and are tied off to the grid or fly floor at the top for safety. Booms can also be fixed to the rear of the proscenium arch or hang from the ends of light pipes. 2) An arm mounted on a microphone stand.

BOOTH
Control Room where the lighting control console and operator are located, as well as possible follow spots and possibly a Stage Manager who calls lighting cues.

BORDER
A horizontal masking piece used to mask the lighting instruments or scenery hanging above the stage from the audience's view. Often used in conjunction with "legs."

BOUNCE
1) To bring in the House Curtain fast, then take it out again immediately.
2) Lighting term describing light beams reflected off the stage or set.

BOX BOOM
A front of house vertical lighting position usually located at the front of an audience seating box.

BOX SET
Naturalistic setting of a complete room built from flats with only the side nearest the audience (the fourth wall) missing.

BREAK A LEG
Say it on Opening night. Say it before any performance. Say it instead of "Good Luck" (which is considered bad luck). You can also even say "Merde" which is French for "shit" but it's OK when it is said as a wish of luck before going on the stage.

BREAKUP
A thin metal disc inserted inside a lighting instrument which gives a textured effect to the light, without throwing a specific pattern onto the stage. A leafy breakup is used for outdoor scenes in forests etc. to break up the light on the actor's faces. Also called "Gobo."

BREAKOUT
A pigtail connection at the end of a multi-cable which allows several other cables to be connected and run in different directions.

BRIDGE
A walkway which provides access to technical and service areas above the stage, auditorium or linking fly-floors.

BROADWAY
The name of a street but also the name of the theatre district in New York. The highest level of theatrical enterprise in the U.S.

BUMP
A flash or sudden jump in light level (a snap cue).

BURNT OUT
1) The lamp inside a lighting instrument has stopped working.
2) A colored gel that has lost its color or melted due to excessive heat in front of a light.

BUS and TRUCK
A theatrical tour designed for short stops, usually 1 to 4 nights.

BUSINESS
A piece of unscripted or improvised action, often comic in intention, used to establish a character, fill a pause in dialogue, or to set a scene. An author may simply suggest "business" to indicate the need for some action at a certain point in the play.

—— C ——

C-CLAMP
A device used to easily and quickly clamp or hold 2 or more items together in place of nails or screws for the purposes of quick release. Made of iron in the shape of a "C" with a tightening rod that closes the opening, thereby pinching the items to be held together.

C-WRENCH
Abbreviation of Crescent Wrench, named for the curved shape of the tool. An electrician's primary tool.

CABLE
1) Wiring, temporarily rigged, to carry electrical current. Depending on the size of the cable (current carrying capacity), cables are used to supply individual lights, whole dimmer racks, or carry signals from a microphone etc.
2) Steel braided wire used, among other things, to hang scenery above the stage.

CALL
1) A notification of a working session (i.e. a Rehearsal Call)
2) The period of time to which the above call refers. (i.e. "Your call for tomorrow night's show is 7:30 pm")
3) A request for actors to come to the stage (i.e. "This is your places call for Act 1.")

4) The Stage Manager on the book is "calling the cues" - the process of giving verbal cues to the lighting, sound, fly men and stage crew during the performance.

CALLBACK
Performers that are being considered after the first audition are asked to audition a second time. Callbacks can happen more than once as the field of possibilities is being narrowed.

CANS
A euphemism for any headphones.

CANVAS
Used to cover flats as a less heavy alternative to plywood.

CAST
The performers who will perform the roles in the production.

CASTING
The process by which the director along with other casting people choose the performers who will perform the roles in the production.

CATWALK
An access walkway to equipment.

CENTER LINE
Imaginary line running down the stage through the exact center of the proscenium opening. Marked as CL on stage plans. Normally marked on the stage floor and used as a reference when marking out or assembling a set.

CHAIN HOIST
Manually operated or electrically driven hoist for lifting scenery and lighting equipment. Commonly used to lift lighting trusses into position for touring shows or concerts.

CHANNEL
A designated control slider which controls lighting or sound equipment. Can be computer or manually controlled.

CHASE
A repeated sequence of changing light levels.

CHEAT SHEET
A smaller version of the full lighting plan, used by the lighting designer during the lighting of a show. A quick reference guide to all the lighting equipment.

CHEWING THE SCENERY
An actor who gives a completely hammy and over-the-top performance is said to be "Chewing the Scenery."

CHINAGRAPH PENCIL
A usually white, wax-based pencil used for marking identifying numbers on lighting gels and the ends of long lengths of cable. Also used for marking magnetic tape prior to splicing.

CHOREOGRAPHER
Member of the production team responsible for setting dances and movement sequences during the production.

CHORUS
The ensemble of vocalists and dancers who support the principal performers in onstage. May understudy one or more principal roles.

CIRCUIT
1) The outlet into which a lighting instrument is connected to a dimmer or patch panel - numbered for reference.
2) A complete electrical "loop" around which current can flow.

CLEARING STICK
A long, often bamboo, rod used to rescue flying objects or to prevent them from becoming entangled.

CLEAT LINE
Rope passed through alternate cleats on two adjacent flats to hold the flats together.

CLOVE HITCH
Invaluable knot that every technician should know.

COLOR CHANGER
1) Scroller: A long string of up to 16 colors is passed horizontally in front of a light. Remotely controlled by the lighting operator.
2) Wheel : Electrically or manually operated disc which is fitted to the front of a light with several apertures holding different color filters which

can be selected to enable color changes. Mainly used inside moving light instruments.

3) Magazine : Manual semaphore-type device used to drop color in place on the front of a follow spot.

COLOR FRAME or Gel Frame
A frame which holds the color filter in the guides at the front of a light. Many different sizes of frames are needed for the different lighting instruments.

COMPANY MANAGER
Member of the producer's team with duties that are directly related to the members of the company, such as: check distribution, ticket orders, hotel or transportation bookings, etc.

COOKIE
See Gobo.

COUNTERWEIGHT
A standard weight (60 or 30 lbs.) used in a counterweight flying system.

COUNTERWEIGHT SYSTEM
Method of flying scenery which uses a cradle containing weights to counterbalance the weight of flown scenery. Sometimes called an "arbor system."

COVE
The front of house catwalk lighting position.

CRASH BOX
Box of glass or other debris used for creating sound effects.

CREW
Term covering all those who work backstage on a show.

CROSS
The movement of an actor across the stage in any direction.

CROSS FADE
The transition between lighting cues. Also applies to sound effects or music. Sometimes abbreviated to X-fade or XF.

CROSSOVER
A route leading from one side of the stage to the other, out of the view of the audience.

CUE
The command given to technical departments to carry out a particular operation. Normally given by stage management, but may be taken directly from the action (i.e. a Visual Cue).

CUE LIGHT
System for giving technical staff silent cues by light. Ensures greater precision when visibility or audibility is limited.

CUE SHEET
A list showing the cues in correct order as they are to be carried out.

CUE TO CUE
A purely technical rehearsal where the action and dialogue between cues is eliminated, to save time and address technical elements.

CUEING
There is a standard sequence for giving verbal cues :
   "Stand-by Sound Cue 19" (The words "Stand-by" come first)
   "Sound Cue 19 Go" (The word "Go" comes last).

CURTAIN
1) The drapery which separates the stage from the audience.
2) The action of the House Curtain coming down at the end of an Act or the play.

CURTAIN CALL
When the acting company comes on stage to receive their applause at the end of the show.

CURTAIN LINE
An imaginary line across the stage that represents where the main curtain would fall. Actors stand behind this line during a curtain call so the curtain doesn't hit them on the head when it is lowered.

CURTAIN TIME (Curtain Up)
The beginning of the show.

CYCLORAMA (usually just "cyc")
A white cloth or plastered wall covering the rear of the stage. Maybe curved at the ends. Used to effect the distant sky which then can be colored by a mixture of light to resemble dawn through sunset.

—— D ——

DANCE CAPTAIN
The assistant to the choreographer on a show who is responsible for maintaining the choreography after the chorcographer leaves.

DARK
A venue that has been closed to the public because there is no current production being offered.

DEAD
1) Scenery or equipment not needed for the current production.
2) An electric circuit that has been switched off or has failed

DEAD HANG
To fly a relatively lightweight item without a counterweight.

DECK
1) Stage Floor. 2) Audio tape machine.

DEPUTY
An elected member of the acting company who is responsible for upholding the rules set forth by Actors' Equity.

DESIGNER
Person(s) responsible for the different visual aspects of the production. Separate designers may be employed for scenery, costumes, lighting etc.

DIALOGUE
The spoken text of a play – the conversations between characters.

DIFFUSION
See FROST.

DIMMER
Electrical or electronic device which controls the amount of electricity passed to a light, and therefore the intensity of the illumination.

DIALOGUE
The lines or words spoken by the cast in a show.

DIMMER RACK
A number of individual dimmer circuits mounted in a cabinet for easy transport and access.

DIRECTOR
The person charged with the ultimate responsibility for the interpretation of the script in production through his control of the actors and crew.

DOLLY
A small wheeled platform used to move heavy items.

DONUT
A metal disc with a hole in the middle inserted in the front guides of a lighting instrument. Used to sharpen focus or reduce spill.

DOOR SLAM
A small wooden box with a hinged lid, or a wall mounted door with various bolts and locks, used to simulate slamming and other door sound effects offstage.

DOUBLE HANDLING
Moving scenery and other equipment more than necessary because it wasn't properly sorted or positioned in the first place.

DOWNSTAGE
The part of the stage nearest to the audience (the lowest part of a raked stage). So named from early theatre when stages were sloped upwards away from the audience.

DOWNLIGHT
A light from directly above the acting area.

DRAMATIST
A playwright, composer or lyricist who takes an existing story and transforms it into a play or musical.

DRAPES
Stage Curtains. See also TABS.

DRESS PARADE
A review by the director, designer & wardrobe staff of all costumes worn
by the cast and seen under stage lighting.

DRESS REHEARSAL
A (hopefully) non-stop full rehearsal, with all technical elements brought
together including costumes. A "final dress" is usually performed in front
of family and friends just prior to paid public performances.

DRESSER
Stage crew personnel who help actors with costume care and costume
changes during the performance.

DRESSING (the set)
Decorative props (some practical) and furnishings added to a stage
setting.

DROP
Painted cloth hung perpendicular to the stage and used as a backdrop.

DRY ICE
Frozen solid carbon dioxide (CO_2) at a temperature of -87.5 degrees
centigrade which produces clouds of steam forming a low-lying mist or
fog when dropped into boiling water. Dangerous: do not touch.

DRY TECH
A practice run of technical cues or the scenery & lighting changes of the
show, usually without actors.

—— E ——

EDISON PLUG
Standard domestic power connector in the USA.

EFFECTS PROJECTOR
Lighting instrument used to project an image from a rotating glass effects
disc. Commonly used discs are clouds, flames and rain.

ELECTRICS (LX)
The department in the theatre responsible for stage lighting and sound and maintenance of the building's electrical equipment.

ELEVATION
A working drawing usually drawn to scale, showing the scaled view of a set or lighting plan. See PLAN.
The term "elevation" refers to a Front elevation. A Rear elevation shows backs of scenic elements. A side view of a set is known as a "section."

ELEVATOR STAGE
A type of mechanized stage which can be raised or lowered.

ELLIPSOIDAL
A lighting instrument with an elliptical reflector and at least one lens. Generally throws a narrow beam of light.

ENTR'ACTE
An "overture" to begin the second part or act of a performance.

ENTRANCE
1) A part of the set through which actors can walk onto the stage.
2) The act of an actor walking onto the stage.

EPILOGUE
A section of the play, or speech to the audience by an actor, after the formal action of the play is concluded.

EQUITY
See ACTORS' EQUITY ASSOCIATION.

ESCAPE
A means for an actor to get on or off of a high level of stage scenery out of view of the audience. Usually steps. Can be a ladder.

—— F ——

FADE
A lighting or sound change either up or down.

FADER
The control knob or slide that provides the means of controlling the output level of a light or a sound amplifier.

FALSE PROSCENIUM
A frame formed by scenic canvas or a vertical flat within the proscenium arch. Used to reduce the size of the opening when putting a small set onto a large stage.

FALSE STAGE (SHOW DECK)
A special stage floor laid for a production to allow scenery pieces, guided by tracks cut into this false floor, to be moved by steel cables. A false stage is also required for putting a turntable into a stage.

FAR CYC
Lighting instrument used to light upstage cycloramas or drops.

FIRE CURTAIN
The heavy fire-proof curtain that, in an emergency, is dropped at the front of the stage, sealing the stage from the auditorium and thus slowing the spread of flames.

FIRE PROOFING
Treatment given to fabric, wood, drapes etc. to retard flammability. Many scenic materials require regular re-application of fire proofing treatment to maintain safety.

FIRST PIPE (FIRST ELECTRIC)
The lighting pipe immediately upstage of the proscenium arch.

FLAT
A wood or metal frame covered with muslin canvas or plywood. A "rail" is the horizontal battens within a flat. A "stile" is a side or vertical piece within a flat.

FLIES
Extension of the stage walls and roof upward which allow scenery to be flown up until it is out of sight of the audience. The ideal fly height should be more than twice the height of the proscenium arch.

FLOOD
1) A lensless light that produces a broad non-focused spread of light. Floods are used to light cycloramas or large areas of the stage or scenery.

2) To increase the beam size of a focus spot by moving the lamp and reflector towards the lens. "Flood that a bit, please !"

FLOOR PLAN
See GROUND PLAN.

FLOORCLOTH
A canvas covering for the floor of the stage. The cloth can be painted to resemble some surface, and be easily removed to reveal another cloth or the stage floor below.

FLOOR POCKET
A electrical socket mounted under a flap in the stage floor.

FLOWN
Scenery that has been attached to the counterweight system and is able to be hoisted into the flies.

FLUFF
To hesitate - to nearly forget or fumble one's lines.

FLY FLOOR(S)
High working platform or floor at the side(s) of the stage from which the flying lines are handled. Often are also the sites for dimmer racks for connecting lighting cables to dimmers. Also called Fly Loft.

FLY MAN
Crew person (stagehand) who operates the counterweight fly system.

FOCUS
The direction and sharpness of each lighting instruments, angled toward scenery or acting areas.

FOCUSING
The process of setting or readjusting the direction and sharpness of the lighting instruments.

FOG MACHINE
See SMOKE MACHINE.

FOH
See FRONT OF HOUSE.

FOLLOW SPOT
A powerful lighting instrument usually fitted with its own dimmer, iris, color magazine and shutters, mounted at the sides or rear of the auditorium, operated by a stagehand so that the light beam can be moved around the stage to follow an actor. Sometimes another instrument may be used in the same way from a position above the stage.

FOOT
1) The action of bracing the bottom of a ladder when it is climbed.
2) Holding the bottom edge of a flat with your foot while a colleague raises the flat from a horizontal to a vertical position.

FOOTLIGHTS
A compartmentalized lighting unit sometimes recessed into the front edge of the stage.

FORESTAGE
That part of the stage which projects from the proscenium into the auditorium. See Apron.

FOURTH WALL
The imaginary wall which separates the audience from the stage in a proscenium theatre.

FREEZE
To stop all action and movement on stage, usually during applause or just before a lighting cue.

FRESNEL
A type of spot light containing a lens with a set of concentric circular ribbings on its surface. Gives a wide even field of light with soft edges.

FRONT OF HOUSE (FOH)
1) Every part of the theatre in front of the proscenium arch. Includes audience seats, lobbies, foyer areas, rest rooms – any area open to the general public.
2) All lights which are hung on the audience side of the proscenium and are focused towards the stage.

FRONT OF HOUSE STAFF
The house manager, ticket sellers, ticket takers, ushers, concession and merchandise people.

FRONT TABS
House curtains.

FROST
A diffusing filter used to soften the edges of a light beam.

FX
Abbreviation for "Effects," usually referring to Lighting or Sound
Effects, but can also mean special stage effects.

—— G ——

GAFFER'S TAPE
Sticky cloth tape. Most common widths are ½" for marking out areas and
2" (usually black) for everything else. Used for temporarily securing
almost anything.

GEL or Gelatin
The thin translucent filter material place in front of lighting instruments
to create a colored illumination. Color filters can be made of glass or
gelatin, hence Gel, but today are usually made from a synthetic plastic
material.

GHOSTLIGHT
1) A light left burning overnight on stage to keep friendly spirits
illuminated and unfriendly spirits at bay. Also to stop people tripping
over bits of scenery when they enter the theatre in the dark.
2) Also refers to the light emitted by a lighting instrument when a
dimmer has not been "trimmed" or calibrated correctly, and is leaking.

GENIE
(Trade Name) A range of mobile access platforms or lifting devices with
either hand-cranked or compressed air lifting mechanisms.

GLOW TAPE
Luminous yellow self-adhesive tape used to mark floors so that positions
can be found in blackouts.

GO
The action word used by stage managers to cue other technical
departments. The word GO shouldn't be spoken by others on headsets

(especially when the crew is on STANDBY) as they may assume it's the stage manager speaking.

GOBO
A thin metal disc with cut-out patterns, which can then be projected by a lighting instrument (i.e. Foliage, Windows). Also called "Pattern" and "Cookie" (short for Cucaloris from the Greek kukaloris: the breaking up of light).

GREASEPAINT
Name refers to make up supplied in stick form, for application to the face or body. Needs special removing cream.

GREEN ROOM
A room adjacent to the stage for the actors to meet and relax. Green, the color, is also known to be psychologically soothing.

GRID
The support structure above the stage on which the pulleys of the flying system are supported. Grid is short for GRIDIRON.

GRIDDED
Any flying piece raised as high as possible into the flies. A scenery piece that has reached the grid, is said to have been gridded.

GROUND PLAN
Scaled plan showing the exact position (as seen from above) of walls and doors and electrical outlets, and indicating the position of items that are suspended above.

GROUNDROW
1) A long low piece of scenery positioned at the base of a backdrop or cyc used to mask the bottom of the cyc or the lights lighting a backdrop.
2) Compartmentalized floodlight units at floor level used to light the bottom of sky cloths or cycs.

—— **H** ——

HALF HOUR CALL
Call given to the actors half an hour before they will be called to the stage for the beginning of a performance. Subsequent calls given are the

"fifteen" at 15 minutes, "five" at 5 minutes and "places" at 3 minutes before curtain up.

HAND PROP
Any prop handled by an actor.

HANGING
Attaching flying pieces of scenery to the appropriate battens.

HEAD ELECTRICIAN
See MASTER ELECTRICIAN

HEAD CARPENTER
The senior member of the carpentry crew. Oversees the carpentry crew and all facets of the shows daily carpentry/scenic operation.

"HEADS"
A shouted warning for staff to be aware of activity above them. Also used when an object is being dropped from above.

HEADSET
1) General term for theatre communication equipment.
2) A headphone and microphone combination used in such communications systems with a belt pack.

HEMP
A type of rope used for flying, made from fibers braided together.

HEMP SET or SYSTEM
The simplest flying system consisting of a series of hemp ropes threaded through pulleys on the grid, and tied off on the fly floor on a cleat. A theatre using a hemp flying system is known as a Hemp House.

HIGH HAT
See TOP HAT

HOOK CLAMP
A clamp with a wing bolt for hanging a light on a horizontal lighting pipe.

HOT SPOT
An area on the stage where the lighting is unintentionally more intense than in other areas. Corrected by lowering a light level.

HOUSE
1) The audience ("How big is the house tonight ?")
2) The auditorium ("The house is now open.")

HOUSE LIGHTS
The auditorium lighting which is commonly faded out when the performance starts. Can be controlled by a dimmer located on the stage or in the light booth behind the audience.

HOUSE MANAGER
The manager of the theatre. The person in charge of the Front of House staff.

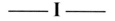

I.A.T.S.E.
International Alliance of Theatrical Stage Employees. The Stagehands and Wardrobe Union. Each city has a different Local Chapter. (In New York stagehands are Local #1; Wardrobe is Local #764.)

IN
Flying term for bringing down anything that has been flown above the stage.

INCANDESCENT LAMP
The typical light bulb. The light results from the bright glowing of a thin thread of metal (the filament) when an electrical current is passed through it.

INTERCOM
Usually refers to microphone/speaker communications equipment used for communicating between various rooms or areas of the theatre. Used to call the actors to the stage.

IRIS
An adjustable circular diaphragm used to alter beam size in an ellipsoidal spot. Made up of a set of interleafing plates. When rotated the small hole formed by the plates opens or closes.

JUMPER
An adaptor from one type of electrical connector to another.

JUMP SET
A second version of the set used on tour to give the advance crew extra time to set up in the next venue.

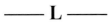

KEY LIGHT
The primary lighting for an area, or person.

KILL
To switch off (a light/sound effect); to strike/remove (a prop).

KLIEGL BROTHERS
The oldest stage lighting manufacturer - founded 1896 in New York.

— L —

LADDER
Non-climbable structure in the shape of a ladder from which lights can be hung in a vertical "stack." Used in the wings for side light.

LAMP
The light source within a light, but also used to refer to the complete unit.

LAMP CHECK
The visual systematic checking of each light before each performance in case any lamps require replacement.

LAMP FOCUS
Knob on a light used to adjust the alignment of the lamp to the reflector and thereby creating either soft or hard edges to the light image onstage.

LASH
To secure side-by-side flats with rope. The rope is known as a Lash Line.

LAVALIERE MICROPHONE
A small microphone that can be clipped or attached to a performer's clothing or hidden in the performer's hair.

LIGHT LEAK
1) Light that is emitted from holes around the lighting instrument. Corrected by using noncombustible "black wrap" to block the leak.
2) Voltage from a badly adjusted dimmer that causes lights to be on when they should be off (ghosting).
3) Any light that can be seen through scenery or curtains or backdrops.

LD
Lighting Designer.

LEGS
Drape set as masking piece at the sides of the acting area. Usually set up in pairs across the stage and used in conjunction with borders (overhead) to frame the audience's view.

LEKO
A type of ellipsoidal lighting instrument which includes an iris for focusing the beam of light into a narrow beam. Named after Joe **Le**vy & Ed **Ko**ok - founders of Century Lighting in the USA.

LIBRETTO
Text of opera, or other long musical vocal composition. The script of a musical.

LIFT
The orchestra pit and/or sections of the stage which can be raised or lowered by hydraulics. Sometimes called "elevators."

LIGHTING EFFECTS
Any manipulation of light or lighting instruments (by rotating pattern discs) that produce movement of light onstage.

LIGHTING PLAN (PLOT)
A scale drawing detailing the exact location of each light used in a production, in relation to the stage area and/or the scenery. Includes any other pertinent information (i.e. its dimmer number, focus position and

color number). Used as a map by the master electrician to "hang" the show's lighting instruments.

LIGHTING DESIGNER (LD)
The person responsible for designing and executing the lighting design for a production, including everything having to do with lights – their types, positions and intensity.

LIGHTING REHEARSAL
Sometimes called a "cue-to-cue" where there are no actors present and the scenery is moved on and off the stage, scene-by-scene, so that the lighting designer can set light levels and light cues.

LOAD-IN
The process of moving set, props, costumes and other equipment into a theatre as well as hanging & focusing the lighting equipment, building the scenery and generally preparing the theatre for the running of the show on a daily basis.

LOAD-OUT
Striking all of the props and lights and sets etc. and moving the entire production out of the venue, either into a large trash container, into a storage warehouse or into a truck for touring.

LOCKING RAIL
In a counter weight system the rail which runs the length of the counterweight wall frame fashioned with rope locks that the ropes pass through. Prevents rope slippage and movement of any hanging item.

LYRICIST
Author of the words of a song.

—— M ——

MAKING THE NUT
The 'nut' is the break-even point for a show. It's calculated on a weekly operating expense basis. All income above the weekly nut is split between investors. Some costly shows don't fully pay back investors and make a profit until well into the run – if ever.

MARKING OUT (SPIKING)
Sticking tape on the floor of the rehearsal space to indicate the ground plan of the scenery. Also for marking position of furniture etc. within a set.

MASKING
Neutral material or designed scenery which defines the performance area and conceals the technical areas.

MASTER
1) An overall control on a lighting or sound control board. The Grand Master takes precedence over all other controls.
2) An original (i.e. Master tape, Master plan) which should be used only to make a copy.
3) A Department Head (i.e. Master Carpenter, Master Electrician, Prop Master).

MD
See MUSICAL DIRECTOR

MASTER ELECTRICIAN
The senior member of the lighting crew. Sometimes called "Head" Electrician. Oversees the lighting crew and all facets of the shows daily lighting operation.

MIC
(pronounced "Mike") Abbreviation for microphone.

MICROPHONE
Device for converting sound into electrical pulses which can then be amplified through speakers or recorded onto tape.

MIME
The art of portraying characters and acting out situations or a narrative by gestures and body movement without the use of words; pantomime.

MIRROR BALL
A large plastic ball covered with small mirror pieces. When a spotlight is focused onto the ball, specks of light are thrown around the room. Usually motorized to rotate.

MONITOR
1) An onstage speaker which allows a performer to hear the output of the PA system, or other members of a band.
2)   A video display screen.

MUSICAL DIRECTOR
The conductor/leader of a musical, or the person responsible for the musical content of a production.

 **N**

NATIONAL TOUR
Tours of Broadway shows to major cities in the U.S. Usually stays in each city for several weeks or months. Show values are similar to the original Broadway production. Salary minimums and Union rules apply.

NOTES
Where the director (or production stage manager) makes comments to members of the cast or crew after a show about the good and bad points of the show.

 **O**

OFF BOOK
The actors have memorized their lines and don't need to read from or "carry" the script anymore. Opposite of On Book.

OFF-BROADWAY
Theatre in New York, outside of the Broadway area, where commercial theatre is produced. Limited to 499 seats. Union contracts apply.

OFF-OFF-BROADWAY
Theatre in New York, outside of the Broadway area, where non-commercial theatre is produced with independent or grant funding. Limited to 99 seats. Union contracts do not apply.

OFFSTAGE
1) The direction towards the nearest side of the stage from the center.
2) The area out of sight of the audience

ONSTAGE
On the main stage acting area, or a movement towards the center of the stage from the sides.

OPEN
To turn or face in the direction of the audience.

OPENING NIGHT
The first public performance after previews when the critics publish their reviews.

OPEN THE HOUSE
Clearance given to FOH staff by stage management that the stage is set and the audience can enter and take their seats. Usually accompanied by a backstage announcement: "The House is now open."

ORCHESTRA
1) The musicians who play the musical score to a show.
2) The ground floor seating in an auditorium.

ORCHESTRA PIT
The sunken area in front of the stage where the orchestra plays during a performance.

OUT
In flying: up (out of sight). In lighting: lights off (blackout).

OUT FRONT
1) The area in and around the audience.
2) Looking towards the audience.

OUTRIGGER
An extendible leg used to increase the stability of equipment (i.e. Genie Lift, Scaffold tower).

OVERTURE
The music which begins a performance.

—— P ——

P & R
Picture and resume. The "calling card" of actors given to directors or agents with the actor's credits and personal information on the back of an 8x10 glossy photo.

PAGING
1) The act of holding a tab etc. open to allow large scenery or prop items or actors to move on or offstage.
2) Preventing microphone or lighting cables from getting tangled by pulling on or guiding them as equipment is moved.

PAN
Movement of lighting from side to side.

PANCAKE
Basic make-up item, available in a range of shades.

PAPER THE HOUSE
The marketing technique of giving away tickets to a performance (i.e. Previews) to make a show seem to be selling better than it actually is, and to start generating "word of mouth" interest.

PARCAN
Type of lighting instrument which holds a par lamp. The parcan is the basic lighting unit in concert lighting.

PARALLEL
1) The folding frame that forms the base of a portable platform.
2) The opposite of SERIES when referring to wiring two loads into one outlet.

PASS DOOR
A fire-resisting door in the wall of the proscenium arch which is the only direct access between the auditorium and the stage without walking on the stage.

PATCHING
Connecting lighting or sound equipment to dimmers or circuit boards with electrical cables.

PERIAKTOI
Greek term for three-sided flats mounted on a rotating base. Used in rows to produce easily changed backings.

PIANO DRESS
Rehearsal in costume and with all technical elements but using a piano as a substitute for orchestra, so that the director can concentrate on technical problems rather than musical ones (and not pay the orchestra!).

PIN SPOT
A lantern focused very tightly on a small area (i.e. an actor's head).

PINK NOISE
Random audio noise containing all frequencies in the audio spectrum. Used to set equalization equipment for a large PA installation. Also called White Noise.

PIPES
The horizontal steel tubes hung from flying lines from which lighting equipment and scenery etc. may be suspended. Sometimes known as a Batten. Also known as a Boom when standing vertical on a large steel weighted base.

PIT
Usually, a lower section between the front of the stage and the audience (or under the apron) where the orchestra sits. It can also describe any area around the stage where the musicians sit.

PLACES
The opening positions for actors at the start of the show (or act).

PLAN
A scale drawing showing a piece of scenery, lighting layout etc. from above.

PLOT
List of details and actions required of technical crews during the performance (i.e. Sound Plot, Light Plot).

PRACTICAL
Any working stage apparatus (i.e. light switch or television). An electrified prop.

PRE PRODUCTION
Phase of production before actors rehearse (or sometimes have even been
cast) and before sets are built. Brings together the production team to
plan and budget the production.

PRESET
1) Anything in position before the beginning of a scene or act (i.e. Props
placed on stage before the performance, lighting state on stage as the
audience are entering.)
2) An independently controllable section of a manual lighting board
which allows the setting up of a light cue before it is needed.

PREVIEW
1) Public performance of a show prior to Opening Night.
2) A function on some memory lighting control desks with video
monitors which enables the operator to see the levels of dimmers and
other information in a lighting cue other than what is on stage.

PRINCIPALS
The actors in a show with the lead or speaking roles.

PRODUCER
The person responsible for raising the financing to mount a show and
then generally running the business side.

PRODUCTION DESK
Table in the auditorium at which director/designer etc. sit during
rehearsals (especially technical rehearsals). Usually have lighting and
communication hook-ups.

PRODUCTION MANAGER
Oversees all technical preparations, including budgeting and scheduling
of a productions technical aspects. See TECHNICAL DIRECTOR.

PRODUCTION STAGE MANAGER (PSM)
The Head of the Stage Management team comprised of the Stage
Manager (SM) and Assistant Stage Manager (ASM).

PROLOGUE
Speech or scene presented to the audience before the start of the Show.

PROMPT
The act of feeding an actor her lines if she can't remember.

PROMPT BOOK
Master copy of the script or score, containing all the actor moves and technical cues, used by stage management to control the performance. Sometimes known as the Production Book or "book."

PROMPT DESK
The stage manager's control center for the show. Contains: a clock, low level lighting, a flat surface for the prompt book, communication hook-up to other technical departments, a phone for emergency, rear and front of house call system and cue light controls.

PROPPING
The task, usually performed by the Prop Master or his assistant, of going around finding / borrowing / buying props for the production.

PROP MASTER
The person in charge of all of the properties on a show including building, procuring and maintaining them.

PROPS (Properties)
Furnishings, set dressings, and all items large and small which cannot be classified as scenery, electrics or wardrobe. Props handled by actors are known as hand props, props which are kept in an actors costume are known as personal props.

PROP TABLE
Table in convenient offstage areas on which properties are stored for each performance and to which they should be returned after use.

PROSCENIUM ARCH
The opening in the wall which stands between stage and auditorium in some theaters. The "fourth wall."

PROSCENIUM THEATRE
Any theatre that has a proscenium arch.

PUBLIC ADDRESS SYSTEM
The auditorium sound system.

PUBLICITY
The production department whose job it is to advertise the show and
entice the audience into the theatre.

PYROTECHNICS (Pyro)
Chemical explosive or flammable firework effects with a manual
detonation. All pyrotechnics should be handled by licensed technicians
with close reference to local licensing laws, and the manufacturer's
instructions.

QUICK CHANGE
A change of costume that needs to happen very quickly and takes place
close to the side of the stage. Costume designers need to know about the
need for a quick change so that the costume is constructed incorporating
elements such as Velcro and zippers rather than buttons.

QUICK CHANGE ROOM
Area adjacent to the stage containing lighting, a mirror and a costume
rack in which actors can make costume changes quickly, sometimes with
the aid of a dresser.

RAG
Euphemism for a curtain or fabric drop. Can refer to any curtain hanging
onstage.

RAKED STAGE
A sloping stage which is raised at the back end, away from the audience
(hence the term 'upstage'). Early theaters were built with raked stages for
better viewing because the audience seating was on a flat surface.

READ-THROUGH
Reading the script out loud from beginning to end so the actors can get to
know their characters and see how the story unfolds.

REHEARSAL
Learning the show by the cast and crew before public performance.

REPERTORY
A theatre company, usually with a permanent company of actors, where two or more shows are running in the same theatre on an alternating daily or weekly schedule.

RESUME
A list of past theatre experiences used by any theatre person to summarize their background.

RETURN
Flats joined to the downstage edge of a set or unit that extend or "return" into the wings. They help mask and also keep the downstage edge of a set from looking raw.

REVEAL
A return which is at right angles to a flat, and suggests the thickness of a window, wall, doorway etc.

REVOLVE
A turntable built into the stage floor on which scenery can be set and then rotated into view either manually or electrically with a motor drive. A revolve can also be built on top of an existing stage or platform.

RIDER
Any special information or requirement attached to a standard contract that sets out specific details pertinent to a particular actor, venue or show.

RIG
1) The construction or arrangement of lighting equipment for a particular production (noun).
2) Installing lighting, sound equipment and scenery for a show (verb).

RISER
1) Any platform on stage.
2) The vertical portion of a step which gives a set of treads its height.
3) A microphone which can be raised through a small trap in the stage floor to a convenient height for an actor.

ROAD CASE
A strong, rigidly constructed, well padded case used to protect equipment from the abuse of touring.

ROAD MANAGER (ROADIE)
A technician with touring shows or music groups who is responsible for the unloading and setting up (tuning etc) of the musical, sound or lighting instruments.

ROYALTIES
The contracted fee paid to an author, designer or director, or their agents for the performing rights of a play and the work involved in mounting it.

RUN
A sequence of performances of the same production.

RUNNERS
1) Persons employed as production assistants to do odd jobs and errands during a production period.
2) Strips of carpet used backstage to silence Actors' shoes during performance.

RUN THROUGH
A rehearsal at which all the elements of the production are put together in their correct sequence and hopefully run non-stop.

—— S ——

SAFETY CHAIN
Chain or wire fixed around lights and lighting pipes or booms to prevent danger in the event of failure of the primary support (e.g. Hook Clamp). A requirement of most licensing authorities.

SAND BAG
A canvas bag filled with sand used to secure and weight scenery on the stage.

SCENE DOCK
High-ceilinged area on the stage, opening onto the street or large elevator, through which the scenery and other equipment in loaded into the theater.

SCENE NIGHT
The new Off-Off-Off-Broadway type theatre event where actors get
together and present scenes for public display. Used for the expression
and stretching of the craft as well as possibly to attract agent interest.

SCENE SHOP
Open room where scenery is constructed. Often shortened to 'Shop'.

SCRIM
1) Cloth with a relatively coarse weave. Used unpainted to diffuse a
scene played behind it. When painted and lit from the front it becomes
opaque. It becomes transparent when the scene behind it is lit.
2) A fine metal mesh used to reduce the intensity of light from TV lights
without affecting color temperature.

SCOOP
A special type of floodlight consisting of a lamp mounted in a large
ellipsoidal reflector. The body of the instrument is usually circular which
means a soft edged circular beam is produced. Often used as work light
in a theater.

SCROLLER
See COLOR CHANGER.

SET
1) To prepare the stage for action.
2) The complete stage setting for a scene or act.

SET DESIGNER
Member of the artistic team for a show who works with the director to
create the scenic "look" for the stage scenery and any accompanying
props. Also sometimes designs the costumes.

SFX
See SOUND EFFECTS.

SHACKLE
A metal connecting device originally for joining chain, comprising two
parts. An open link connects the items to be joined and a pin is fitted to
make the link complete.

SHEAVE
The wheel in a pulley which carries the wire or rope.

SHIN BUSTER
The lowest lantern on a lighting boom. Named because of the proximity
of sharp parts of the light to the bones of the lower leg.

SHOW REPORT
A written report by stage management noting problems, running times,
show staff and audience numbers for the previous days' performance(s).
Copies are circulated to the appropriate staff.

SHUTTER
Accessory for an ellipsoidal light. Metal blade which can be used to
shape the edge of the beam. Shutters (normally four) are located in the
gate at the center of the light. Similar in effect to barn doors on fresnels.

SIGHTLINES
A series of lines drawn on plan and section to indicate the limits of the
audience vision from extreme seats, including side seats and front and
back rows. Often marked in the wings as a guide to the actors and crew.

SKIN MONEY
Extra payment made to actors when nudity is required on stage.

SMA / S.M.A.
Stage Managers' Association – organized in 1982 to assist stage
managers in their professional careers. Maintains a list of stage managers
available for work and posts jobs for stage managers.
(stagemanagers.org)

SMOKE MACHINE
A Smoke Machine or Fogger is an electrically powered unit which
produces clouds of white non-toxic fog (available in different
flavors/smells) by the vaporization of mineral oil or dry ice.

SMOKE POCKET
A vertical steel channel on the upstage edges of the proscenium arch in
which the edges of the fire curtain travel.

SNAP HOOK
A plastic or metal hook used to hang tabs etc. A sprung catch prevents
the hook becoming detached.

SNAP LINE
Chalked piece of string which, when stretched tight and "snapped" is
used for marking straight lines on stage or on scenery as a painting aid.

SOUND CHECK
A thorough test of the sound system before a performance.

SOUND DESIGNER
Member of the production team who has the responsibility for planning
and executing the layout of all sound playback and reinforcement
equipment for the show. This role also includes the sourcing of music
and sound effects for the production.

SOUND EFFECT
Either recorded or live background sound accompanying the action.

SOUND OPERATOR
Also known as Sound Op. and responsible for operating the sound
playback and mixing equipment for a show. He or she is often a member
of the Electrics department of the theatre and works with the sound
designer for the production.

SPANSET
Woven strap designed to be wrapped around girders and other structural
support points. Has loops at each end to which a shackle carrying a
suspension cable can attach. Available in a number of different loads.

SPOT LINE
A temporary line dropped from the grid to mark where something gets
suspended in an exact special position.

SPECIAL
A light within the lighting plot which is required for a specific moment
or effect within the performance, and is not part of the general cover
lighting.

SPIKE
To mark the position of an item of scenery or furniture, or an actor on
stage.

SPILL
Unwanted light onstage.

SPOTLIGHT
General term for any light with a lens system.

STAGE CREW
Members of the theatre staff who are responsible for moving props and/or scenery, or handling lighting equipment during the show, and for ensuring that items under their responsibility are working correctly and properly maintained. Stage Crew (also known as Stagehands) are often employed on a temporary basis for a specific production, and may not be part of the theatre's full-time staff. They also may be touring with a particular production.

STAGE DIRECTIONS
Directions in the script about how the playwright intends actions or arrangements to be carried out.

STAGE DOOR
The door to the theatre through which the cast and crew enter and exit the theatre. Not the public entrance to the building.

STAGE ELECTRICIAN
Member of the electrics staff whose responsibility it is to set or clear electrics equipment during scene changes. May also carry out color changes on booms etc.

STAGEHANDS
See STAGE CREW.

STAGE LEFT / RIGHT
Left/ Right as seen from the actor's point of view on stage. (i.e. Stage Left is the right side of the stage when looking from the auditorium.)

STAGE MANAGERS
The team responsible for the smooth running of a performance. Before a production opens the stage managers attends rehearsals and meetings with other members of the production team and coordinates all of the various aspects of the production. During the performance the stage manager, using a copy of the script annotated during rehearsals, cues the actors and the various technical departments. The stage managers (particularly the PSM) maintain the artistic quality of the show as well.

STAGGER-THROUGH
The first tentative attempt to run through the whole show. Very rarely runs smoothly, hence the name.

STAND BY
1) A warning given to technical staff by stage management that a cue is imminent. Technicians acknowledge by saying "Standing by."
2) A non-performing understudy for a leading role.

STRIKE
After the last performance, everything used in the production has to be disassembled, packed up and removed from the theater. Some things are thrown away. Some props and sets go into storage to be used again.

SWAG
1) A particularly artistic way of drawing a set of tabs diagonally up at the same time as flying them out. Looks much better than it sounds.
2) Souvenirs given to crew following a particular show or event, usually in the form of T-shirts, posters, & coffee mugs.

SWING
A member of the company of a musical who understudies one of the leads and is also in the chorus.

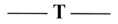

TABS
Any stage curtain including a vertically flying front curtain (house tabs) and especially a pair of horizontally moving curtains which overlap at the center and move outwards from that center.

TAILS
Also known as Bare Ends, and refers to a cable or set of cables with a connector at only one end which is used for connecting a company's equipment directly to the mains supply in a venue.

TEASER
Border, usually black, set behind the proscenium and linked with tormentors to form an inner frame to the stage, and to mask the upper parts of the stage area.

TECHIE
A stage technician or stagehand.

TECHNICAL DIRECTOR
Co-ordinates all technical aspects of the production, from organizing crew calls to ensuring equipment is ordered, to liaising with the designers and sometimes adapting a design to fit the venue. Often shortened to "TD" & sometimes called the PRODUCTION MANAGER.

TECHNICAL REHEARSAL
Usually the first time the show is rehearsed with lighting, scenery and sound. Costumes are sometimes used where they may cause technical problems (i.e. quick changes). Often a very lengthy process. Sometimes called, simply "tech."

THEATRE IN THE ROUND
A stage in which the audience sits on all sides of the stage.

THREE-FER
An adaptor which enables three pieces of equipment to be connected to a single outlet or cable. See also TWOFER

THRUST
Form of stage which projects into the auditorium so that audience members are seated on at least two sides of the extended piece.

TOP HAT
Metal top-hat shaped open-ended tube that can be placed in the slot in front of a lighting instrument to eliminate spill.

TORMENTORS
Narrow masking flats adjacent and sometimes at right angles to the proscenium arch.

TRACK
1) Metal structure with rails on which curtain runners are placed to enable curtains to open and close smoothly.
2) A sideways movement of a flying piece, or flown actor.
3) Separate audio recording channel.

TRAP
An opening through the stage floor.

TRAP ROOM
The area directly below the trapped part of the stage. Used for accessing the traps.

TRAVELLERS
Curtains or scenic pieces moving on horizontal tracks.

TRIM
A pre-plotted height for a piece of scenery or a lighting pipe. Sometimes flying pieces may be given a number of extra trims in addition to the "in (or low) trim" and "out (or high) trim." Trims are marked with colored ribbons fixed into the twists of a fly man's rope.

TRUSS
A framework of alloy bars and triangular cross-bracing (usually of scaffolding diameter) providing a rigid structure, particularly useful for hanging lights where no permanent hanging positions are available.

TWOFER
A two-way adaptor.

U

UNDERSTUDY
An actor able to replace a regular performer when required. May have a smaller role in the show. Sometimes call Standby or "Walking Understudy" meaning not required to be in the theatre but required to be reachable by phone.

UPLIGHT
Light from below the actors - from a light source on the stage floor.

UPSTAGE
The part of the stage furthest from the audience.

UPSTAGING
To deliberately draw focus on stage.

USA 829
The United Scenic Artists Union originally formed in 1897 as the United Scenic Artists Association and re-chartered as United Scenic Artists of

America in 1918. Represents Scenic, Costume and Lighting Designers, Mural and Diorama Artists, Scene Painters, Production Designers and Art Directors, Commercial Costume Stylists, Storyboard Artists and most recently Computer Artists, Art Department Coordinators, Sound Designers, and Projection Designers working in all areas of the entertainment industry.

USHERS
Front-of-House staff who guide audience members to their seats.

V

VARI*LITE
Trade name for a range of "intelligent" moving lights and control equipment.

VISUAL CUE
A cue taken by a technician from the action on stage rather than being cued by the Stage Manager.

W

WAGON
Rolling or tracked platforms or pallets with scenery that are moved into position on stage from storage areas to the side and rear of the main stage. Enables complex scene changes to occur almost instantly.

WALK THROUGH
Rehearsals at which the actors go through entrances, moves and exits to make clear any changes or alterations that may be necessary.

WARDROBE
The general name for the costumes, costume department, its staff and the accommodation they occupy.

WARDROBE PLOT
Actor-by-actor, scene-by-scene inventory of all the costumes in a

production, with a detailed breakdown into every separate item in each costume and every costume change.

WARM UP
Time before a performance during which the actors prepare their bodies through a number of physical, mental, and musical exercises.

WASH
Stage lighting focused on stage not in a specific spot, but more as a general lighting over an area.

WARNING BELLS
Sometimes recorded, sometimes actually rung – by the House Manager or an usher to call the audience back from intermission.

WEST COAST
In theatres with reduced flying height, West Coasting is the act of bundling up a cloth or backdrop and tying it to pipe so that it can be flown out of sight. Originated on the west coast of the US.

WINGS
The out of view areas to the sides of the acting area.

WORK LIGHTS
1) High wattage lights used in a theater when the stage or auditorium lighting is not on. Used for rehearsals or work calls.
2) Low wattage blue lights used to illuminate offstage obstacles and props tables etc. during performance.

WORKSHOP PERFORMANCE
A performance in which maximum effort goes towards acting and interpretation of the script rather than sets or costumes, or the visual performance. Sometimes arranged for potential backers by a Producer looking to produce a full scale production of the show.

—— X Y Z ——

X FADE
See CROSS FADE

YOKE
A "U" shaped steel hanging bracket, attached to a lighting instrument, that permits the unit to tilt up and down from its hanging position.

About the Author

Bo Metzler has been involved in some form of theatre activity for over 40 years. He spent 10 years doing theatre as a pastime in high school, college, community and regional theatre in Ohio. Six of those 10 years were spent at Kent State University as an actor, scenery builder, lighting tech, propman, stage manager, publicity director, writer and director—on over 40 shows—first as an undergraduate math major (of all things!), and then as a graduate teaching assistant working on a Master's degree in theatre and teaching theatre labs.

In 1974 he began a 32 year career in New York where, all in all, he plied his trade on over 2 dozen Off-Off-Broadway and Off-Broadway shows and in over 20 different Broadway theatres on over 30 Broadway shows throughout the years. His work on Broadway has spanned the jurisdiction of 3 labor Unions anywhere from a few days (on load-ins & load-outs) to months and even years on such shows as *La Cage aux Folles, 42nd Street, Jekyll & Hyde, Sweet Smell of Success, The Lion King* and the three longest running Broadway shows: *Cats, Phantom of the Opera and Les Miserables.* (Working on Broadway as an actor, stage manager, dresser, electrician, carpenter and propman may very well be a uniquely singular professional achievement.)

Mr. Metzler has also worked on various TV shows such as 5 years on *Sesame Street* (3 times earning Emmy Certificates for his contribution to Outstanding Lighting Direction), and various sporadic days on *Donahue, Letterman, Today, Later, Jane Whitney, Howard Stern, Jane Pratt, Dudley, Inside Moves and Family Edition.*

He has traveled as a company manager, road manager, stage manager, actor and scenery van driver on three tours throughout the U.S. (once even assisting with hair & make-up); supervised the wardrobe and dressed Harry Belafonte in Canada, Germany, Italy, Spain, Zimbabwe as well as in Vegas, Atlantic City and other U.S. cities; designed for a Modern Dance Company which performed in Israel, South Korea, Japan and New York; worked as a stagehand on 15 rock concerts in Omaha; stage managed or crewed Tributes & Benefits at: Lincoln Center (MET & Avery Fisher), The Waldorf Astoria and Giants and Yankee Stadiums; worked at the CBS carpentry shop, E.L.T., La Mama ETC, the Orpheum, Theatre of the Open Eye, Lion Theatre, Harold Clurman Theatre, The Public Theatre, Manhattan Theatre Club, The New Victory Theatre, The Actor's Studio, The Kennedy Center, The Spoletto Festival and Lincoln

Center State Theatre and was a staff stage manager at the American Academy of Dramatic Arts on more than a dozen full productions.

Mr. Metzler has also worked in Dinner Theatre and Children's Theatre and even helped build houses for Habitat for Humanity. He is the author of a play about the Lincolns entitled "*Abraham and Mary,*" which he appeared in as well as directed, and is working on a new book based on a journal chronicling his last two years on *The Lion King*, tentatively entitled *It's About Ethics, Stupid!*

The author on the prop crew
of his last Broadway show
(2006)

If you enjoyed this book – spread the word!

Give the gift of Theatre!

Infinity Publishing's
"Buy Books on the Web"
www.bbotw.com
(Look under "Performing Arts/Theatre")
(877) BUY-BOOK

Send Comments to:
whatwedocomments@gmail.com

Visit the Website at:
www.whatwedo-book.com

Breinigsville, PA USA
19 May 2010
238377BV00001B/74/P